WHAT PEOPLE ARE S

CYBER DISOB

One thing is clear: the Internet is likely the largest decentralized project in all of human history. Shantz and Tomblin hone in on the Internet's renegades and radicals, who utilize the Internet's unprecedented power for the purposes of resisting authority, creating international solidarity, and spreading the meme of anarchy. *Cyber Disobedience* describes hacktivists, the free software and anti-copyright movements, digital whistleblowing, and other efforts to create a freer and more just future, both online and offline. This book truly captures the rebel spirit at the heart of the Internet Age.

Dana M. Williams, California State University, Chico

Beyond the restrictive and narrow politics-as-usual from both left and right, the authors demonstrate the passionate and creative forces of contemporary anarchism that fly in the face of both corporate media and traditional academic accounts alike that perpetrate the mythical popular image of anarchism as utopic and disorderly. Providing discussions on everything from the rise of Anonymous, the Arab Spring, and demonization of whistleblowers such as Daniel Ellsberg, Julian Assange, Bradley Manning and Edward Snowden, to the coining of the term "hacktivism" in 1998, *Cyber Disobedience* explores the role of social media in information-sharing and movement-building possibilities. Activists, students, scholars—anyone interested in anti-capitalist social movements and digital resistance from below—will benefit from reading Shantz and Tomblin's arguments that are theoretically sophisticated, empirically rigorous and historically significant. A lucid, compelling and provocative account of the potential of the digital revolutionary spirit, the text sets a very high standard for debates in the social studies of power, knowledge and technology. Overall, Cyber Disobedience constitutes a significant and timely contribution— a must-read for anyone concerned with freedom, technology, social justice and state repression in the twenty-first century.

Dr Heidi M. Rimke, Ph.D, Associate Professor of Sociology, The University of Winnipeg, Winnipeg, Manitoba, Canada

Cyber Disobedience

Re://Presenting Online Anarchy

Cyber Disobedience

Re://Presenting Online Anarchy

Jeff Shantz and Jordon Tomblin

Winchester, UK
Washington, USA

First published by Zero Books, 2014
Zero Books is an imprint of John Hunt Publishing Ltd., Laurel House, Station Approach,
Alresford, Hants, SO24 9JH, UK
office1@jhpbooks.net
www.johnhuntpublishing.com
www.zero-books.net

For distributor details and how to order please visit the 'Ordering' section on our website.

Text copyright: Jeff Shantz and Jordon Tomblin 2013

ISBN: 978 1 78279 556 8

All rights reserved. Except for brief quotations in critical articles or reviews, no part of this
book may be reproduced in any manner without prior written permission from the publishers.

The rights of Jeff Shantz and Jordon Tomblin as authors have been asserted in accordance with
the Copyright, Designs and Patents Act 1988.

A CIP catalogue record for this book is available from the British Library.

Design: Lee Nash

Printed and bound by CPI Group (UK) Ltd, Croydon, CR0 4YY

We operate a distinctive and ethical publishing philosophy in all
areas of our business, from our global network of authors to
production and worldwide distribution.

CONTENTS

Webs of Struggle: Introducing Anarchy and Cyber
    Disobedience   1
Cyber Disobedience: Hacktivism and Beyond   4
Organizing Anarchy   7
Of Plastic Guns, Lulz, and Liberty: Two Struggles over
    the Communication Commons   10
And Two on Surveillance   15
Against the Law   18
Uncivil Disobedience?: Beyond Politics as Usual   20

Chapter 1. Re://Presenting Anarchy: Constructing Fear   **22**
Fin de Siècle Fears: Constructing the Anarchist Menace at
    the turn of the Twentieth Century   24
Writing Anarchism All Wrong: Literary Re://Presentations
    of Anarchy   28
Fin de Siècle Fears, Again: The Unabomber and the Dawn
    of the Internet Age   33
A Note on "Terrorism"   36
A Creative Passion   37

Chapter 2. Finding the Middle Ground in Cyberspace:
    A Content Analysis of Hackers in Film   **40**
Method   43
Hacker Portrayals   48
Revolutionary & Political – Shaping the World
Advanced Understanding of Computers   51
Terrorist–Anarchist Enemy of the State   52
Malicious, Harmful Intentions and Fearless of Punishment   53
Fun and Entertainment Seeking

Curiosity   55
Lack of Malicious Intentions   56
Financially Motivated   57
Vengeful

Chapter 3. Sailing the Cyber Sea: Hacktivism and a
    Capitalist Response to Piracy   61

Chapter 4. Applying For Netizenship: Foucault,
    Cybercrime and the Digital Age   75

Chapter 5. Walking the Plank: Inciting Change through
    Whistleblowing   87
Legislative Nodes: Sometimes Conducive, Sometimes
    Disparaging   88
Opaque Webs: Exposing Health and its Consequences   91
Transparency and Heresy: Inciting Change through Struggle   94
Whistleblower Inception and Legal Deception   95
Piracy and Privy: A Tentative Dispute   100
Conclusion   103

Chapter 6. Against the Online Enclosures: For a Cyber
    Commonism   104
On the Commons: Common Resources, Common Struggles   105
DIY Production: Challenging Capital   108
Future Possibilities/Potenza?: Complexity, Networks, and
    Change   111
Control Matters   113
Against Authoritarianism   114
Rethinking Democracy   116
Immediatism: Theorizing Resistance to Enclosure and the
    "One World" of Capitalism   117
Conclusion?   125

For Molly, Saoirse, and p.j. For all who seek anarchy, online and off. (J. S.)

Jordon Tomblin would like to acknowledge his family and best friend, Preeti, for their continuous support over the years. And my eternal gratitude goes to Greg, colleague, supervisor, mentor, and friend.

Webs of Struggle: Introducing Anarchy and Cyber Disobedience

The development and spread of the internet over decades to become perhaps *the* mass medium of the twenty-first century, has been marked by struggles, which have often been hidden behind the screen of cyber mania. Yet these struggles are those that have always marked the development of capitalism, and capitalist means of production from steam to the assembly line to robotization and on—the struggle between producers/consumers and owners.

In the early days of the web, way back in the 1990s, there was great wariness of and opposition to the privatization and commercialization of the internet which was viewed as an important shared resource—a collective consciousness of sorts. Marxist theorists John Bellamy Foster and Robert W. McChesney note that those engaged with the internet worked on the general belief that "[c]ommercialism and an honest, democratic public sphere did not mix. Corporate media were the problem, and the Internet was the solution. Good Internet citizens needed to be on the level; they should not hustle for profit by any means necessary. Although not entirely free and democratic – it was, after all, based on military technology – the early internet was seen by its users as 'theirs'" (2011, n.p.). Indeed early commentators on the developing webworld, such as Richard Barbrook, clearly viewed and identified the internet as a communications commons. Even more, movements of tech activists were seen as commonists (asserting the sharing of web resources and the need for alternatives to capitalist ownership and control but in a way that avoided, or refuted, the authoritarian or statist examples of communism).

At the same time some segments of capital readily grasped the enormous commercial potential of this untapped channel of profitability. To do so fully the cyber commons, like the land commons on England in the late feudal period, would have to be enclosed, brought within the purview of private property owners, as commodities. Many early cyber activists recognized this too and tried to mobilize users and producers to defend the free net and extend the spheres of openness, through tech worker collectives and open source technologies.

Over the last decade, of course, the enclosure of the internet as commercial space has expanded massively. The internet has gone from being viewed as a medium of mass communication or interchange to become a mass market (for exchange value). Corporations have used the internet to advance global trade in an immediate fashion, collapsing space and time for commerce. At the same time corporations have found entirely new commodities and spaces for profit making. As Squire suggests:

> It has allowed a space in which data have become a valuable commodity at the same time as allowing data to be more accessible than ever to potential consumers. Corporations that hope to capitalise on data try to clear out the online commons and subjugate internet users to the ever encroaching profit motive of online companies. In many ways, hacktivism is a response to this contestation of rights. (2013, n.p.)

Despite claims to neutrality and proclamations of disinterested concern for privacy and rules of access, states of all political stripes globally have been highly interested players, intervening to ensure the legal enclosure of the web. Government bills, laws, and treaties have consistently restricted the rights of internet users and tech workers while affirming or asserting special rights of capital (owners and investors who seek a privately commodified web).

Marxist analysts Bellamy Foster and McChesney argue that governments routinely serve the interests if cyber capital over and against users and workers:

In the realm of the Internet, a state-corporate alliance has developed that is matched perhaps only in finance and militarism. It makes a mockery of traditional economics, with its emphasis on an independent private sector responding to a competitive market ... [The] stories of how Amazon and PayPal cooperated with the government in the WikiLeaks affair ... point to the demise of the separation of public and private interests. (2011, n.p.)

Commodification of social resources, of information as for materials or lands, occurs through processes of privatization or enclosure by which access to otherwise available goods or services is restricted by and/or to those who have enclosed or privatized. By rendering goods and services as "private property" they are made relatively scarce or inaccessible. This allows for profit-making by controllers of the resources. Such is the process at the heart of capitalist development from the start, what Marx called so-called "primitive accumulation." Notably, it is the process at the heart of contests over the commercialization, or commodification, of the internet, of information, of the online commons.

As in the case of earlier processes of capitalist commodification, the efforts to commodify the internet or communications commons are being met with resistance. As the enclosures of common lands gave rise to the Diggers, Levelers, and Ranters, communities that took direct action to reclaim the commons, so the efforts to privatize and corporatize the web have given rise to hacktivists and cyber disobedients who take action for a free and open webworld. These new Diggers, Levelers, and Ranters take names such as Anonymous, LulzSec, Riseup, and TAO (The Anarchy Organization).

As in previous periods, the resistance is criminalized by states acting on behalf of propertied interests that profit from enclosure. Cyber disobedients are criminalized because they seek, or succeed, to give away that which capital seeks to own, and sell, for a profit (Squire 2013). Restricting access to readily available information is a way to maintain and extend the commodification of data. And the key way in which this commodification can be achieved is by making information a scarce resource, by limiting its accessibility.

Cyber Disobedience: Hacktivism and Beyond

Cyber disobedience becomes a central means for engaging in action to defend free and open access to information and the sharing of information, the basis of an online commons. As Jo Squire (2013, n.p.) suggests, contemporary hacktivism serves as both an adjunct to more traditional activism on behalf of more familiar issues as well as being a cause in its own right. Perhaps the most notable convergence of cyber disobedience and street demonstrations can be seen in the mass uprisings of the Arab Spring.

The term hacktivism is popularly used to describe a range of activist activities, particularly sabotage or disruption, online. These can range from denial of service (DOS) attacks, involving overwhelming amounts of traffic directed at a website causing the server to overload, to the infiltration of computer systems, taking over websites or other actions in which computer based technologies are means and/or targets for political campaigns or actions generally conceived. On the characteristics of hacktivism, Jo Squire notes an interview with information activist Asher Wolf, a former member of the hacker group LulzSec, who described hacktivism as: "the use of computer hacking, the internet, and technology to try to effect social change or spread a message. It's similar to normal activism except it takes place online. For example, instead of a sit-in, you have a [denial of service] attack. Instead of graffiti, you have website defacements" (quoted in Squire 2013, n.p.). Hacktivism is one action oriented aspect of an overall approach that brings perspectives and practices from more familiar forms of civil disobedience (non-

4

compliance, sit-ins and occupations, trespassing, public witnessing, and so on) to the webworld. This overall approach is one of *cyber disobedience*, merging activism with organizing and movement building—it is an expression of resistance, of disobedience toward institutional authorities.

Cyber disobedience emphasizes direct action, rather than protest, appeals to authority, or simply registering dissent, which directly impedes that capacities of economic and political elites to plan, pursue, or carry out activities that would harm non-elites or restrict the freedoms of people in non-elite communities. Cyber disobedience, unlike much of conventional activism or even civil disobedience, does not restrict actions on the basis of state or corporate acceptance or legitimacy or in terms of legality (which cyber disobedient view largely as biased, corrupt, mechanisms of elites rule).

In many cases recently, people and groups involved in online activism or cyber disobedience are also involving themselves in real world actions and organizing. In other cases people and groups who have only been involved in real world efforts are now moving their activism and organizing online as well.

Many of the people who have participated in cyber disobedience have come to reflect on the relationship of their online actions and movements or campaigns being mobilized in communities, workplaces, and/or the streets. These reflections have led growing numbers to develop strategic or tactical relations with real world organizing and movement activities. As Squire suggests: "This is one of the reasons why Anonymous participated in its own ways in the Arab spring and the Occupy movement, rather than simply dismissing the street protests as 'old' or 'boring,' a common sentiment in online activism" (2013, n.p.). Clearly, this is a rethinking of political action in ways that engage old and new, familiar and unfamiliar. It is a strategic undertaking rather than a pure pursuit of novelty.

We saw such an intersection with Anonymous' response to

the mass uprisings of the Arab spring. In some ways this has also provided a high water mark for cyber disobedience. Recognizing, perhaps too late, the effectiveness of social media, mobile communications, and online alternative media as organizing tools for people in struggle against the Egyptian dictatorship, Mubarak's government moved to shut down the web throughout Egypt. Closing down this vital means of communication posed a real threat to organizers and activists seeking to confront the government, though it should be pointed out that it did not stall the movement which really gained its strength and momentum from face to face discussions and actions in neighborhoods throughout Cairo and elsewhere.

In response to the dictatorship's actions, Anonymous deployed their tech skills to distribute so-called online care packages to people involved in the resistance "on the ground" in Egypt. Zip files containing instructions and phone numbers for dial up access to the internet along with software allowing online anonymity and firewalls were distributed along with other resources by which the governments censorship efforts could be circumvented (Squire 2013).

The so-called care packages greatly assisted the Egyptian organizers and activists to get back on the web. The online organizing tools that had been important resources for the resistance were back in their hands despite the best efforts of a, somewhat clumsy dictatorship. Notably, similar care packages have been deployed since in other uprisings of the Arab Spring and as part of the Palestinian resistance in Gaza (Squire 20103).

This shows the dual character of cyber disobedience. It has a constructive, solidarian, aspect of mutual aid that circulates knowledge among movements in struggle. At the same time it has a confrontational, direct actionist element that can target opponents, even shutting them down in parts.

One thing that is clear is that cyber disobedience in various forms, from basic DOS attacks to major hacks, will continue to grow, with more innovative and more dramatic actions in store. On one hand the cyber disobedients are becoming more proficient and confident. At the same time more people are drawn to online organizing given successes following the Arab Spring and Occupy. Social movements view it as a more regular or everyday aspect of organizing. On the other hand, economic and political elites, states and capital, are ever more present online. They (and their power) circulate online, enclosing much of online "space," so there will be an impetus to confront and challenge them online.

For political organizers and activists, there remain important questions about the tactical and strategic roles of cyber disobedience in social movements (particularly more radical movements against states and capital). Part of this probing requires better understandings of more focused forms of cyber disobedience and their potential contributions to collective, or common, struggles.

Much of cyber disobedience has developed in an engagement with anarchist ideas and practices. At the same time there is much resemblance between cyber activist forms and anarchist approaches to organizing. Yet the anarchist character of much cyber disobedience has been little discussed.

Organizing Anarchy

Commentators have persistently failed to appreciate, or have misrepresented the organizational approaches of cyber disobedients. As internet analyst and author Gabriella Coleman, who has written on Anonymous, suggests:

> Anonymous is not a singularity, but is [composed] of multiple, loosely organised nodes with various regional networks in existence. [But] Operations don't simply spring out of the ether and can be easily linked to a particular network ... At minimum these networks usually will lay claim to, or deny, the source of an operation. (2012b, n.p.)

7

While Anonymous, and other cyber activist groups, and their actions, can appear, from the outside, to be rather chaotic, unorganized, even random, they actually apply a range of organizing practices. As Squire suggests, cyber activist groups have their own internally functional methods of organizing (2013). Often these organizing methods are unfamiliar or recognizable to outsiders, even informed commentators, because they do not pursue the hierarchical, command structures of mainstream political (party) or corporate organizations. They do not have instituted leadership positions or roles, hierarchical structures, or authoritarian (leader/follower, boss/subordinate) command processes. Often decisions are made on a participatory basis in which all involved are able to discuss plans. In other cases there is full autonomy of action such that any member or collective can take action as it sees fit, as long as they are accountable for their own actions. Collectives are often formed on the basis of affinity and trust, so that people work on projects with those they have a direct connection with and commitment to. These organizing practices, from affinity groups to participatory democracy to horizontal structures, are precisely the practices that have characterized anarchist movements historically. Thus whether implicitly or explicitly, as many are, the cyber disobedient represent a form of organizational (if not philosophical) anarchism.

This horizontal, participatory, decentralized organizing is perhaps more in keeping with the desires for personal liberty, authenticity, and action desired by a younger generation of people concerned about social justice. Such organizing provides an opportunity for people who believe their voices have been silenced by status quo politics to actually have a voice. Indeed, even organizational approaches that have marked the political Left up to the present period have tended to be rather hierarchical, even bureaucratic, and representational, whether one refers to social democratic political parties, communist parties, or trade unions. Anarchy has always posed an alternative to such organizational forms within the Left. A central component of anarchist perspectives is the belief that means and ends of politics should correspond. Thus in anarchist political organizing, a radical approach to form can be as important as content.

As various commentators (Squire 2013; Coleman 2012a) point out, cyber activism and activists have drawn considerable media attention over the last few years because they are seen as novel and even a bit exciting. Certainly, cyber disobedience seems a bit more engaging and lively than the rather dour images of political party meetings and campaigns. The association with anarchism further gives them a sense of edginess or mystery that makes them even more appealing to many younger people upset about social injustice and seeking to take action against the status quo. It might be remembered that an earlier generation of young people frustrated with the early manifestations of neoliberal austerity and tired of the worn out forms and symbols of protest, the first wave punk rockers, also found a suitable expression for their outrage in anarchism. From the guttural howl of Johnny Rotten and the Sex Pistols, who proclaimed "Anarchy in the UK" ("I am an anarch-iste), anarchism and punk have been closely associated, the "circle-A" an instantly recognizable symbol of both (and of uncompromising resistance to authority). In the present context, the Guy Fawkes mask of Anonymous (drawn from the graphic novel "V for Vendetta" written by the openly self-identified anarchist Alan Moore), has become the ubiquitous symbol of anarchy (on the web and in the streets, as during Occupy protests and widely since).

The word "anarchy" is derived from the ancient Greek word "anarchos" and means, rather than chaos or disorder, simply "without a ruler." While rulers, not at all surprisingly, promote fears that the end of their rule will inevitably lead to a social decline into chaos and turmoil, anarchists assert that rule, economic or political, is unnecessary for the preservation of order. Rather than a descent into Hobbes' mythical war of all against all, a society without government suggests to anarchists the very context for creative and peaceful human relations. Pierre-Joseph Proudhon, the first to identify positively his social theory as anarchist, succinctly summed up the anarchist position in his famous slogan: "Anarchy is Order" (which is symbolically represented by contemporary anarchists in the "circle-A" or @).

For anarchists, the regulatory and supervisory mechanisms of state capital are especially suited to producing docile and dependent subjects. Through institutions like courts and prisons, but also social work and psychology, authorities extend practices of ruling from control over bodies to influence over minds. Moral regulation, and unquestioned respect for laws, provides a subtle means for nurturing repression and conformity. The results is relations of dependence rather than self-determination as the externalized practices of the state increasingly come to be viewed as the only legitimate mechanisms for solving disputes or addressing social needs. For anarchists the "rule of law" administered through the institutions of the state, typically on behalf of capital, is not the guarantor of freedom, but, rather, freedom's enemy. Such practices close off alternative avenues for human interaction, creativity, and community while corralling more and more people within the bounds of state capital.

Of Plastic Guns, Lulz, and Liberty: Two Struggles over the Communication Commons

In the second week of May, 2013, Cody Wilson of Defense Distributed, a loose collective dedicated to asserting the freedom of information against state regulation, was forced to remove plans for a 3D printed weapon from his website after receiving threats of legal action from the United States Department of State (DoS or State Department). Earlier in the month, Wilson had shocked people in the United States (and many observers across the globe) by creating a fully functional (if not particularly high-powered) plastic pistol using a 3D printer. Before the plans were taken down, though, the blueprint had been downloaded about 100,000 times. It can be found still (as of this writing) on other websites as well as various file-sharing services such as the popular Bit Torrent.

More than wanting to talk about the gun that has stirred up so much public consternation and ire, Wilson has preferred to speak, in often excited terms, about the affirmation of knowledge freedom represented by his boxy derringer (which looks more like a movie camera than a handgun).

Indeed, as much as concerns over the gun itself, an inaccurate, shingle-shot, short-range piece known as "The Liberator," commentators have been troubled by the anarchist tinged perspective of the gun's media massaging, and openly provocative, guru, Wilson. As supposed small government advocate, and former George W. Bush speechwriter, David Frum complained in an article on the implications of The Liberator: "Anti-social behavior will always be with us. It's the accompanying sermons that stick in the craw" (2013, n.p.). For Frum, the 3D gun is simply the lasted in a growing line of examples of the do it yourself (DIY) culture of the internet going deadly.

For Brian Doherty, writing in the December 2012 issue of *Reason* magazine, Wilson's experiment "bears down on the techno-anarchy, 'information wants to be free' aspect of 3D printing, straining it possibly to its breaking point by grounding the grand promise of decentralized cheap ways to make ideas physically real in something as troubling as weapons" (n.p.). Doherty, who also identifies the impetus for a communication commons as anarchy, is less bothered by the gun and its advocate Wilson than is Frum. Nor does he express the outrage over the real subject of the ongoing debates over the 3D peashooter, which is, after all, not guns but anarchy (or freedom beyond the state).

It is perhaps highly telling that in a socio-historical period of the real subsumption of society by a military metaphysic debates over freedom and liberty hide behind discussions of weapons. Even more telling that in a period of mass murder delivered from the skies by "unmanned" drones piloted by video gamers, all hostility and social anxiety is reserved for a single shot plastic zip gun.

In moving against Wilson, the State Department chose openly to violate Wilson's First Amendment rights, those protecting free speech, and arguably his Second Amendment right to bear arms. This confirms a point that all anarchists make, and have always made—that state-sanctioned rights are subject to withdrawal whenever the state decides (especially if it feels threatened). They are untrustworthy rights indeed.

The "free market" (it has never been free) defender Frum sees the potentials of 3D printing not as a liberation of free information, but as a theft of copyrighted material. In this he expresses one side, the side of privatization, in the age old struggle over commons and enclosure. As Jesse Kline suggests:

> This is not the first, or the last time we'll see governments struggle to adapt existing regulatory regimes to new technological innovations. But it will always come down to a simple choice: Create massive censorship apparatuses that have varying degrees of success (such as the great firewall of China) or come to the realization that overbearing government intrusions in our lives have become as obsolete as a ColecoVision games console at a garage sale. (2013, A12)

This is only one in the long list of attempts by government to clamp down in panic fashion on new technological developments. As Kline reminds us: "When the Pretty Good Privacy (PGP) encryption protocol was released in 1993, the State Department targeted it for allowing people to communicate without the threat of government surveillance. But it was already too late: PGP's source code was readily available and it became the basis for a host of other technological advances" (2013, A12). Cyber disobedience and the pursuit of communications commons overflow, and outpace, attempts at enclosure, not always, but often.

In the case of Defense Distributed and their 3D marvel, as in other cases before and since, before the State Department could act, the file had already escaped—or been liberated. Once the plans were out, people, as they will do, set to work and began collaborating on improving the design. As Jesse Kline suggests: "The free sharing of information spurs innovation" (2013, A12). It also calls into question existing capitalist regimes of property ownership and control and the relations of production that privilege those who claim (rights to) value (as profit) over those who actually produce value. As is the case with much of cyber disobedience, what is really being challenged is a capitalist mode of production in which knowledge and the people who create it are rendered as commodities.

At the same time as the US State Department was violating Cody Wilson's First Amendment rights, a court in Britain was sentencing four young hackers to 32 months in prison for cyber attacks on a range of elite targets (economic and political) including prominent ones such as the Central Intelligence Agency (CIA), the United Kingdom's Serious Organized Crime Agency, the US Air Force, Sony Picture, 20th Century Fox, and Rupert Murdoch's News International. The cyber disobedient also hit the Arizona State Police and tech security firm HBGary Incorporated.

The means of attack was the Denial of Service (DOS) attack overwhelming the sites with traffic. The sentenced were associated with groups LulzSec (from LOL, or laugh out loud and security), a fraction that splintered from the amorphous collective Anonymous years before. The cyber disobedient had constructed a bitnet—a network of computers to perform the

DOS attacks on the various websites. The chief executive officer of HBGary resigned following the attacks. It is believed that the companies experienced serious financial damage.

From the perspective of cyber anarchy the targets are understandable. All represent powerful interests socially and all have sought, in various ways, to privatize, to enclose the communications commons. All have also funded, supported, or carried out efforts to criminalize so-called hackers, information sharers, and/or cyber disobedients. For cyber anarchists, the DOS attacks are simply politics by other means. The impact on billion dollar companies and state agencies is minimal compared to the harms inflicted on society by those institutions and agencies targeted. One might remember in all of this that all the cyber disobedients actually did was visit publicly available websites. That they did so in a way that corporations and state agencies did not approve of does not alter that fact but it does, again, raise questions about who gets to be active on the internet (and who only gets to consume), under what circumstances, and according to whose rules (or fees).

At the heart of these cases is the fundamental question concerning the role of government (and what is meant by government, what type of government) in the Internet Age. As Jesse Kline points out: "Most Westerners applaud the Internet's subversive nature when it is used against authoritarian regimes, as it was during the Arab Spring. But the decentralized nature of the Internet can just as easily be used by people in the West, a fact that really irks those who think the government should be in the business of keeping people safe from themselves" (2013, A12). The flows of disobedience connect across space and time and across ideologies.

As Kline concludes: "And here's where we see the true brilliance of what Wilson is doing. No one is saying that shooting people is shouldn't be illegal. But simply making and possessing a weapon is not about equating "gunplay with liberty…It's about

14

sending a message to lawmakers that they can't ban objects or ideas, just because some people find them objectionable" (2013, A12). In this case, the people finding disobedience and the free sharing of information online (and off) to be objectionable have particular economic and political interests. They belong to capital and the state. In various ways and through diverse means they are attempting to ban anarchists and anarchist ideas — movements of and for collective labor and the commons.

And Two on Surveillance

In the first days of June, 2013, a perhaps even more ominous event garnered global attention and generated popular outrage in a way that the censorship of the 3d gun plans and the LulzSec sentences only hinted at. Documents leaked by whistleblower (a key aspect of cyber disobedience), and CIA contractor, Edward Snowden during the first week of June revealed that the National Security Agency (NSA) in the US has compelled US phone and internet companies to turn over the metadata on millions of American customers *every day* for years. The information release by Snowden showed an expansive program of cyberspying on a massive scale by the US government.

The secret surveillance program PRISM has the NSA gaining information from multinational tech corporations, including Google, Skype, Microsoft, Apple, Facebook, and more—a who's who of tech capital. This is the telelectronic convergence of state capital in the form of a world historic surveillance apparatus.

That same week information was revealed about a surveillance program in Canada, the supposedly more liberal state, which collects data on personal communications. The classified program, which collects Canadian internet and phone metadata, was approved by the Defense Minister, Peter McKay, and had been running for several years at the time it was uncovered. Notably, the program was, and remains, so secret that the Office of the Privacy Commisioner of Canada, which oversees government privacy issues, knew nothing of it.

The metadata collection program is managed by an electronic eavesdropping agency, the creepily named Communications Security Establishment Canada (CSEC), which was formed during the Cold War to spy on communications involving Communist states (Freeze and Wingrove 2013, A4). The processes for acquiring metadata by CSEC are not known even by members of parliament. A bipartisan initiative, the first CSEC meta-data directive was signed by the Liberal government in 2005. It was renewed by the Conservative government in 2011.

Before early June of 2013 few people had ever heard of, or knew anything about, metadata. It certainly was not an everyday concern. Yet it should have been and after the Snowden release it has become so for many. As security analyst Ronald Deibert suggests, meta-data is something of a "digital biometric tag" (2013, A11). Meta-data on a cell phone could include the numbers you call, the time and length of the call. It could also include IP addresses of websites you visit.

The electronic pulse of a cell phone emits an electronic pulse every few seconds to the nearest cell phone tower or wifi router, even when not in use. In these pulses are the model of phone, its OS, the location of the phone, and its user (Deibert 2013, A11). Taken together these pieces of data provide a clear picture of a person's life. Deibert reports: "MIT researchers who studied 15 months of anonymized cellphone metadata of 1.5 million people found four 'data points' were all they needed to figure out a person's identity 95 per cent of the time" (2013, A11). It provides a potential goldmine for state spies and corporate marketers alike.

As Deibert notes, this metadata does not simply evaporate. Rather "it moves through the filters and chokepoints of the Internet, and sits indefinitely, there to be mined, on the servers of the companies that own and operate the infrastructure: the telecommunications and Internet service providers like AT&T

and Verizon in the United States, and Bell, Telus and Rogers here in Canada" (2013, A11). And vast resources have been devoted to the tasks of mining.

> Access to metadata, when combined with powerful computers and algorithms, can also allow entire social networks to be mapped in space and time with a degree of precision that is extraordinarily unprecedented, and extraordinarily powerful. Once analyzed, metadata can pinpoint not only who you are, but with whom you meet, with what frequency and duration, and at which locations. And it's now big business for that very reason. A growing complex of top secret data analysis companies orbit the law enforcement, military, and intelligence communities offering Big Data analysis, further driving the need for yet more data. (Deibert 2013, A11)

The NSA has built an enormous new $1.2 billion facility in Utah to handle and process the data. Estimates are that it can process around one hundred years worth of all of the world's communications (Deibert 2013, A11). CSEC too has new $900 million headquarters in Ottawa right next to the Canadian spy agency (Canadian Security and Intelligence Services, CSIS) headquarters. Interestingly, the CSEC complex does not show up on Google maps (Deibert 2013, A11).

These programs amount to constant, ongoing surveillance of people without suspicions, cause, or justification. Wire tap warrants would never be approved by the courts under such circumstances.

Under cover of the "war on terror" governments have been monitoring the personal, private communications of their citizens. The invasions of privacy have occurred with no public or parliamentary debate or discussion and with no limits or parameters on how, when, or what is collected, who gets to see it and how long it can be held by governments. Indeed, in those cases in Canada where the wholesale collection of private data has been debated publicly, public opinion, and mobilization, has killed proposed legislation (*Globe and Mail* 2013, A16).

Behind the banner of security and war (on terror, on piracy, on whatever is needed for political ends) the public is not permitted to know. The public is told to trust the spooks. Responsible people are said to be in charge. "Trust us," they say. "Information is gathered only to stop the bad guys," they promise. But who watches the watchers? Who really calls the shots? Who determines the threat? It is all a state-capital secret.

In the 1950s, the sociologist C.W. Mills warned of a power elite of unelected military, corporate, and state managers who really called the shots and made the fundamental decisions in society *behind* the screen of democracy. They were the actual power-holders in society, the ones who determined political policy, not the elected officials who provided the face, or rather the mask, of democratic governance. Power and authority are wielded from an unacknowledged and unaccountable network.

Notably, Mills argued that this power elite (or military-industrial-complex to use the term popularized by Eisenhower) views the world and everything in it according to a military metaphysic. All of society is, for the power elite, a war zone in which rules of war apply. Social issues are viewed as acts of war—requiring and justifying a military response—complete with a suspension of civil liberties. States of exception rule everyday life—martial law becomes law. A little loss of liberty or privacy is a small sacrifice to be kept safe—a fair tradeoff for security in a time of perpetual war.

Against the Law

It should be noted that the attempts to criminalize, and demonize, cyber disobedients have not been the only manifestations of government efforts to target and halt resistance or break up oppositional groups and actions in the current period. Since the emergence and spread of the alternative globalization movements in the global North during and following the Seattle protests that shut down the meetings of the World Trade Organization, governments in various neoliberal democracies, including the Canada, Britain, the Netherlands, Italy, and the US, have enacted a range of policies and practices to restrict or eliminate street protests (see Shantz 2012). State efforts have ranged from the openly repressive and violent, including the use of tear gas, rubber bullets, water cannons, armored vehicles, and mass arrests, to the legislative, including legislative absurdities like laws against the wearing of masks of any kind during protests.

In this repressive context many activists in liberal democracies have concluded simply being present in the streets is treated as a criminal act during times of protest. This has been borne out in recent protest events like Miami, London, Toronto, and Athens. During the time of the protests against the G20 meetings of global elites in Toronto in 2010, more than a thousand people were subjected to the discredited practice of kettling, in which all people on the streets in an area are rounded up in side streets by police and forbidden to leave. They are all then arrested, regardless of their actions, reasons for being there, or demeanor or perceived threat. Under such circumstances activists have come to question the value, efficiency, or legitimacy of civil disobedience as a means to voice dissent, let alone to effect any real social change.

As some suggest, when protest becomes criminal, only criminals will protest. Some activists have concluded that the only means by which to stop harmful corporate or government practices is, not by appeal to the conscience of economic or political elites who seem, in any event, to have no conscience, or to shame them, they also seem to have no shame, but rather to act directly to make it impossible to carry out their plans. This is the approach advocated by anarchists. The approach of direct action—on the streets, or online.

This direct action impetus characterizes cyber disobedients acting in the webworld. Such direct action has long been a manifestation of producers, going back to the earliest working class, or syndicalist, movements against capital rather than of "citizens" or dissidents or protesters as the civil disobedience of the streets has been.

Uncivil Disobedience?: Beyond Politics as Usual

Cyber anarchists deploying practices of cyber disobedience affirm a break with everyday politics. They refuse the norms that govern political consensus. In particular, they reject notions taken up by much of the political Left (even as alternative globalization movements grow) that revolutionary politics, radical social transformations, are no longer possible. While union leaders and even community activists, who should know better, scream for legality of protest, and seek to comfort police and politicians with apologies for direct action or anti-corporate property damage, the cyber disobedients identify legality as what it is—the screen that hides and protects power. In this their analysis coincides with the works of critical criminologists who have pointed out that legal systems and the police have always been mechanisms of elite rule and class domination. Shantz (2010b) notes that the modern police were conceived to maintain people in their station and roles within a social hierarchy. Numerous commentators, including those in Shantz (2012), have analyzed evolving policing practices during protests as efforts to halt dissent and protect global capital. Cyber disobedients reject Leftist defeatism, despair, and deference to authority—the obedience of the movements.

Struggles, in fact, can, and do, shift the context in which political norms are understood. As Corcoran suggests: "In times when the count of the state is unchallenged, the effective ontological closure means that the sphere of politics will always *consensually* appear to be localized in the State, as a matter of looking after the affairs of the 'political community'" (2011, xiv). Activists must contest and challenge, rather than accept and extend this fake and false consensus. Even more than this, anarchists have always rejected the limitation of the realm of politics to the terrain of the state.

The cyber struggles of the twenty-first century have changed the context for understanding politics and political norms, not only of action but of outcomes. They have helped to dissolve longstanding perspective and practices of politics.

The stakes in the struggles over the communications commons are massive. The outcome will determine whether free and open access to knowledge is maintained and expanded as a shared social resource, or whether knowledge will become further privatized and commodified, accessible only to those who can pay the price demanded by capital. In some ways this is a struggle over the development of state capitalism. As a consequence of the enormous stakes in play, it is perhaps predictable that states and capital have launched a range of offensives, ideological and material, against proponents and defenders of the communication commons.

On the one hand this offensive has been carried out through legislative and repressive means, such as criminalization of cyber disobedience and laws restricting access. On the other hand have been ideological campaigns designed to portray cyber anarchists and hacktivists not as political actors or community advocates but as terrorists. In many ways the current demonization of cyber anarchists echoes the demonization of anarchists carried out a century ago in the various "red scares." These politicized processes of demonization and negative labeling are examined in the next chapters as they have applied to anarchists historically and cyber disobedients today.

Chapter I

Re://Presenting Anarchy:
Constructing Fear

In the middle of the nineteenth century, during the heat of the revolutionary wave of 1848, Karl Marx and Friedrich Engels famously wrote of the revolutionary spectre haunting the combined powers of Europe. That phantom was none other than the spirit of socialism, which at the time was (a fact generally forgotten) largely an anarchist one. Today, in the twenty-first century, while the ghost of Marxist communism has been exorcised (thanks largely to the monstrous failures that took the name of Communism in the various Soviet or Stalinist regimes), the old and seemingly vanquished revolutionary spectre is once again haunting culture and politics—this time by its proper name, anarchism. Since the early 1990s, even before the rise of the alternative globalization movements in the global North would make anarchism a household word again, anarchism as a self-aware force has enjoyed a rather stunning resurgence. Indeed, the resurgence of anarchism has paralleled the emergence of cyber activism. Both have struck a chord with a new generation of organizers and activists seeking an alternative to state capitalism but wary of the limitations and pitfalls of previous forms of progressive radicalism, whether Leninist centralism in organization or activist protest in practice.

While anarchism and cyber disobedience have struck a resonant, and hopeful, chord with people seeking to challenge social injustice, they have been met with rather more negative reactions from corporate mass media. Few social groupings have stirred such an aggressive response from authorities as anarchists who are often presented as synonymous with another great scourge of the twenty-first century, terrorists. In the past few years condemnatory media coverage of angry, black-clad, balaclava wearing demonstrators mobilizing outside of the global meetings of government and corporate power-holders, such as the International Monetary Fund (IMF) or World Bank (WB) has raised memories of the moral panic over anarchism which marked the beginning of the twentieth century. The "uncivil" disobedience, especially where it concerns damage to corporate property, attributed to so-called "black bloc" anarchists at global capitalist summits since the 1999 World Trade Organization (WTO) meetings in Seattle have landed anarchists squarely in the headlines, and crosshairs, and put them on the covers of a range of mainstream media, from the *New York Times* to the *Toronto Star*. It has also garnered them feature stories in various television programs, both as news and as entertainment. In addition, police assaults on anarchists during economic summits, including subjecting them to pepper spray, tear gas, rubber bullets and mass arrests, as well as shootings and even killings, have suggested, with little nuance, to the general public that anarchists are a force of chaos and disorder to be feared. That view has been reinforced in mainstream media depictions of anarchists as little more than "thugs" and "hooligans."

The fact that public conversations about anarchism have been dominated by states and mass media, which uniformly portray anarchists as violent, destructive, even terroristic, means that there has been a lack of informed analysis of anarchist politics. One consequence of this obscuring of the discussion is that the actual perspectives, desires, and visions of this major, and growing, contemporary movement remain largely misunderstood. Lost in recent sensationalistic accounts are the creative and constructive practices undertaken on a daily basis by anarchists simply seeking to develop a world free from repression, oppression, and exploitation. While an examination of constructive anarchist visions, which provides examples of politics grounded in everyday resistance, offers insights into real world attempts to radically transform social relations in the here and now of everyday life, authorities prefer that this constructive aspect of anarchy remain hidden. The discursive attempts to construct anarchists as social deviants is not too surprising given that authorities typically attempt to portray perceived threats to their authority and privilege in a negative light. Indeed, cultural history in the global North shows longstanding efforts by states and mass media to stir public fear and outrage against anarchists who are rendered as monstrous.

Fin de Siècle Fears: Constructing the Anarchist Menace at the turn of the Twentieth Century

The persistent image of the anarchist as violent malcontent or terrorist emerged from a period of social movement desperation in the last decades of the nineteenth century. Following a period of state terror unleashed after the brutal repression of the Paris Commune in 1871 and the extermination by the state of hundreds of working class activists and organizers, some radical activists turned to individual acts of vengeance against perceived agents of the ruling classes. The result was a series of high profile attempted and completed assassinations of politicians and industrialists in North America and Europe.

Mounting frustration with the lack of progressive social change, the continuing conditions of poverty and exploitation for the working classes, and the often brutal violence directed against unionists and striking workers led some to turn towards more aggressive strategies of insurrection. The term "propaganda of the deed" became part of public discourse during this period to describe acts of violence carried out against the wealthy and politicians. Perhaps the most infamous moment during the period came on September 6, 1901 when an unemployed worker and anarchist Leon Czolgosz assassinated President William McKinley. In Europe the most impactful among these was the bomb heaved into the House of Parliament in France by one anarchist by the nom de plume of Ravachol. There were also a variety of public acts of violence against symbols of capitalist society, especially supposed bourgeois clubs and other cultural establishments in which elites were believed to pass the time. Most notable among these was the bomb tossed into a busy café by Emile Henry.

These episodes of *attentat* provided rich fodder for petit bourgeois commentators and novelists of the day and led to the development of a subgenre of literature on anarchist assassin that titillated a generation of anxious readers in an early period of "war on terror" panic. Curiously, the anarchist bomber myth has served as creative inspiration for some of the finest novels ever written in the English language. Prime works include: *The Man who was Thursday* by G.K. Chesterton, *The Secret Agent* by Joseph Conrad, *The Princess Casamassima* by Henry James, and *The Bomb* by Frank Harris. It says something, too, that such prominent authors have turned their energies to writing about the specter of anarchy.

The *fin de siècle* panic over anarchism was not limited to Europe. The social struggles of the late 1800s and early 1900s gave rise to often intense, and highly charged, public discussions of anarchism. In the US, government efforts to criminalize social resistance culminated in the passage of an immigration law of 1903 that sought to prohibit anarchists from entering the US (Hong 1992). As Hong (1992, 111) notes: "The anarchist was the constructed devil of the American civic religion of the late nineteenth century. It was made the bogeyman to guard the borders of the political allegiances, loyalties, and obedience of American citizens." The first North American anarchist Red Scare introduced a durable theme in American political life, not only as a justification for state ideologies and the construction of capitalist social consensus, but also to express and institute acceptable features of American political culture as elites desired them (Hong, 1992, 110). This was a process that Hong identifies as (creating and) caging the anarchist beast that forms the opposition to state capitalism.

The popular portrayal of the anarchist as terrorist made a comeback in North America in the period of the Red Scare of 1919. Indeed, most have forgotten that, despite the impact of the Russian Revolution of 1917, that Red Scare was targeted not at Communists but at anarchists and syndicalists (or anarchist unionists). The Red Scare and the state repression enacted under the Palmer raids, initiated by Attorney General Mitchell Palmer, which included the deportation of foreign born activists, decimated the radical movements of the day, in particular the anarchists and the Industrial Workers of the World. Indeed, in some ways, these movements never recovered to reach the levels of influence and achievement they previously enjoyed.

The trope of anarchist monstrosity has been particularly prevalent during periods of great social upheaval, as characterizes the present period. The era between the first Red Scare and the second Red Scare of 1919 was one of intense social conflict and dislocation as social relations and values were highly contested. As Hong suggests:

> Lurking behind the attack on one kind of revolution of social relations was a different revolution: the appropriation and concentration of power in corporate capitalism and in the strong nation-state. A common interest with the ideology of the latter revolution was cultivated in inverse proportion to the anxiety created about the challenger. (1992, 111)

During the various red scares the image of the anarchist was deployed in a manner that prefigures the official response to anti-globalization movements today. According to Hong:

> The symbolic anarchist enemy came to personify the challenge of anti-capitalist ideas and values. It was constructed to evoke

associations that fostered dependency on authority, freezing political perceptions and conceptions within an acceptable framework. By putting the 'anarchist beast' beyond the pale, it kept citizens within the fold. (1992, 111)

While some have claimed that the period of globalization has been marked by a decline in the nation state, it is more accurate to suggest that within the present period states have responded to social transformation through the exertion of a strengthened nation-state and of values that support it (in new laws, military mobilizations, trade agreements, and so forth).

As Hong (1992, 110) suggests the first Red Scare against anarchists, which marked the beginning of an American political tradition, is significant "because it produced an evocative condensation symbol that has retrained its power into contemporary use. An excess of democracy can still be discredited as the threat of impending anarchy." The anarchist beast remains, even a century after it was supposedly vanquished, a key ideological symbol in hegemonic efforts to legitimize state or corporate discourses and practices. This is, perhaps, especially so in the face of growing opposition movements against capitalist globalization and for a global commons.

As anarchists have noted, such characterizations of organizing and resistance will always be put forward by corporate media regardless of the presence or threat posed by any actual anarchists. This is a lesson also learned by media historians:

The intensity of Red scares far exceeds the actual threat the scapegoat groups represent. This makes sense, insofar as the primary object of these campaigns is not to defeat the weak and resourceless enemy but to win favor for elements within the governing elite and to accomplish the ideological rearmament of a population. (Hong 1992, 127, n. 4).

At the same time, anarchists, as well as many media analysts, also recognize that corporate media are not forums for explaining complex issues. Neither are they venues for positively presenting anti-corporate sentiment. Yet, the corporate media are not the only ones to get anarchism wrong, misrepresenting the movement to the public.

Writing Anarchism All Wrong: Literary Re://Presentations of Anarchy

The literary presentation of the anarchist as a fanatic is most forcefully, and artistically, provided by Joseph Conrad in his great work *The Secret Agent*. In Conrad's telling, the supposedly "anarchist" Professor is actually a Spencerian, a social Darwinist, who seeks a world where only "the fittest" survive—the complete antithesis of anarchism. The weak, he rants, are simply the "source of all evil" (Conrad 1967, 243). His prescription—an actual horror to nonfictional anarchists—is to exterminate all of them. In the vile words of the Professor:

> They are the multitude. Theirs is the kingdom of the earth. Exterminate, exterminate! That is the only way of progress. It is! Follow me Ossipon. First the great multitude of the weak must go, then the only relatively strong. You see? First the blind, then the deaf and dumb, then the halt and the lame — and so on. Every taint, every vice, every prejudice, every convention must meet its doom. (Conrad 1967, 243)

Another potent, and more humorous, portrayal of the shadowy figure of the anarchist is provided by G. K. Chesterton in his wonderful *The Man who was Friday*. There the anarchist is a mysterious, even spectral, figure who moves within secret global networks. This is actually the image of the underground terrorist network. The vision of the anarchist as nihilist is extended in a passage in which Inspector Syme, on the trail of anarchists, speaks with a police officer. The officer, referring to the anarchist conspiracy's inner circle, relates to Syme the anarchist vision as he understands it:

> They are under no illusions; they are too intellectual to think that man upon this earth can ever be quite free of original sin and the struggle. And they mean death. When they say that mankind shall be free at last, they mean that mankind shall commit suicide. When they talk of a paradise without right or wrong, they mean the grave. They have but two objects, to destroy first humanity and then themselves. That is why they throw bombs instead of firing pistols. The innocent rank and file are disappointed because the bomb has not killed the king; but the high priesthood are happy because it has killed somebody. (Chesterton 2007, 46–47)

For the anarchists, as described by Chesterton, even thought is like a bomb. This is expressed by the anarchist Secretary (!), in his argument for the new method over the simpler and more direct form of the knife attack:

> The knife was merely the expression of the old personal quarrel with a personal tyrant. Dynamite is not only our best tool, but our best method. It is as perfect a symbol of us as is incense of the prayers of the Christians. It expands; it only destroys because it broadens; even so, thought only destroys because it broadens. A man's brain is a bomb,' he cried out, loosening suddenly his strange passion and striking his own skull with violence. 'My brain feels like a bomb, night and day. It must expand! It must expand! A man's brain must expand, if it breaks up the universe. (Chesterton 2007, 67)

Another version of the anarchist as mysterious fanatic appears in *The Princess Cassamassima* by Henry James. This grand novel, the most literary of them all, set in Victorian London is peopled with characters drawn directly from the London anarchist community of the day. The titular character, despite the gender change, is a representation of the anarchist prince Peter Kropotkin himself— the expatriate noble who abandons a life of privilege to take up the cause of the oppressed. A portrayal of Johann Most, the most notorious figure of Victorian anarchism is offered in the form of the immense man of mystery, Diedrich Hoffendahl. The leader (!) Most (Hoffendahl) is portrayed largely as a calculating instrumentalist:

> He had exactly the same mastery of them that a great musician — that the Princess herself — had of the keyboard of the piano; he treated all things, persons, institutions, ideas, as so many notes in his great symphonic massacre. The day would come when — far down in the treble would feel one's self touched by the little finger of the composer, would grow generally audible (with a small sharp crack) for a second. (1977, 295)

The anarchist revolutionaries are represented as addled and murderous, seeking only terror and the slaughter of the rich. Anarchism is described as "an aggressive, vindictive destructive social faith" (1977, 18). Anarchists are "the stupid and the blind" who play a part in the career of the protagonist Hyacinth Robinson (James 1977, 10). As if this is not enough, the anarchists are also shallow but earnest (certainly a deadly combination). Take this description of the dreary performance of anarchists at their (inevitably) secret meetings:

> There were nights when a blast of imbecility seemed to blow over the place and one felt ashamed to be associated with so much crude fatuity and flat-faced vanity. Then everyone, with two or three exceptions, made an ass of himself, thumping the

table and repeating some phrase which appeared for the hour to constitute the whole furniture of his mind. (James 1977, 243)

These all too familiar caricatures are portrayed sloppily despite the evidence of years of tireless and selfless organizing among anarchist communists to develop collective ownership and free exchange in relationships of peace and goodwill. Only a cursory study of anarchist activities in London would have made this obvious to James. On the other hand, state order is beautiful, for James, and the protagonist, his values so shallow and fickle, is drawn to withdraw from his revolutionary beliefs by romantic love.

Once again the anarchists (despite their contempt for hierarchical authority) are said to have a headquarters (James 1977, 294). In other words the portrayal is the antithesis of all anarchist organizing in the real world. For the unfortunate protagonist, the anarchist simply follows orders:

He shouldn't judge, he should simply execute. He didn't pretend to say what good his little job might do or what *portée* it might have; he hadn't the data for appreciating it and simply took upon himself to believe that at headquarters they knew what they were about. The thing was to be part of a very large plan, of which he couldn't measure the scope — something that was to be done simultaneously in a dozen different countries. (James 1977, 294)

On the extent of anarchist conspiracy, James writes in raging terms:

'It's beyond anything I can say. Nothing of it appears above the surface; but there's an immense underworld peopled with a thousand forms of revolutionary passion and devotion. The manner in which it's organized is what astonished me. I knew that, or thought I knew it, in a general way, but the reality was a revelation. And on top of it all society lives!...In silence, in darkness, but under the feet of each one of us, the revolution lives and works. It's a wonderful, immeasurable trap, on the lid of which society performs its antics.' (1977, 290–291)

The opinions of the anarchists on public matters are accused of being "poisoned at the source" (James 1977, 19). Anarchism is said to be only one corner of the "'shady' underworld of militant socialism" (James 1977, 18). Never mind the sharp anarchist criticisms of socialism and the heated debates between anarchists and socialists over philosophy and strategy.

Within the portrayals offered by Chesterton, Conrad, and James there are certain caricatures that are repeated, despite the quite different styles and moods of each. Revolution is presented as conspiracy. Its actions are dynamite and assassinations rather than the mundane community and workplace organizing undertaken daily by anarchists. Anarchists are presented as impotent and desperate. On the whole the anarchist conspirators made up only "a little band of malcontents" (James 1977, 245). Social inequality and oppression, the motivating factors behind anarchist organizing to end injustice, are presented merely as excuses. In *The Princess Cassamassima* the protagonist is drawn into a commitment to serve the cause at the possible cost of his life. His cause, the supposed anarchist cause, though, is that of a murderous fanatic: "Very likely it would be to shoot someone — some blatant humbug in a high place; but whether the individual should deserve it was not one's affair" (James 1977, 294). James refers melodramatically to the "sinister anarchic underworld, heaving in its pain, its power and its hate" (James 1977, 21). In each case the esteemed authors have no direct familiarity with the subject matter—the people who might make revolution—and no attempt is made to gain real understanding of them.

In these portrayals the anarchist was uniformly a shadowy

underworld figure predictably attired in black trench coat, black hat pulled low, with a cartoon bomb (bowling ball with lit fuse) under his cloak. Often the anarchist figure was portrayed, interestingly, in a manner currently used to describe the anarchist tech geek. Of course, Anonymous has self-consciously taken up this representation in its own imagery today.

Anarchists, then as anarcho-techies now, have been portrayed as socially awkward, of questionable hygiene, hanging out in the darkness of subcultural joints and back rooms where they engage in obscure discussions of arcane that they pursue obsessively. Often, too, those discussions were of a technological nature. For the trench coat bomber (note allusions to the so-called Trench Coat Mafia of the Columbine massacre) of the nineteenth century, the discussion was bomb making—for the contemporary cyber anarchists, the making of cyber bombs.

As is illustrated in a following chapter, many of these same tropes have been carried forward in contemporary representations of hackers and other techtivists in modern media—particularly in Hollywood film representations. With the mania over the "war on terror" in the twenty-first century, there has been a great renewal of interest in the era of *attentat* of the late nineteenth century. Recent books on the topic include various works of fiction and non-fiction. Some examples include:

The Dynamite Club by John Merriman; *Blood and Rage* by Michael Burleigh; *Murdering McKinley* by Eric Rauchway; and *The President and the Assassin* by Scott Miller.

Fin de Siècle Fears, Again: The Unabomber and the Dawn of the Internet Age

In the late 1990s the figure of the anarchist terrorist made a brief, if spectacular, reappearance in national headlines in the United States. The cause was the rather dramatic police hunt for the so-called Unabomber, the mysterious, even mythic, figure sought by authorities for decades over a series of bombings targeting researchers and corporate figures associated with advanced technological development. Eventually the police hunt would lead to the arrest and conviction of Ted Kaczynski, a once well-regarded Ivy League scientist.

The Unabomber served as an almost perfect condensation point for mounting social fears over rapid technological change and the zeitgeist of anxiety pointing toward a sense of social-technical collapse in the panic of system failure that would manifest most spectacularly (and futilely) in the Y2K phantom. This zeitgeist of anxiety over broad technologically driven social and cultural transformation was expressed by social theorists like Ulrich Beck in the notion of the "risk society."

The Unabomber came complete with a pseudo-anarchist manifesto that touched upon a wide range of late twentieth century concerns over hyper technologization and the associated domination and destruction of the natural world upon which the advanced technological infrastructure rests. In addition to the destruction of nature (and human communities as well) by technology—and the authoritarian structures of state and capital that drive technological expansion, the Unabomber Manifesto identified various threats to human development, on personal and social levels. Indeed, the Unabomber attacks were holistically aimed at an entire technological civilization and the supplanting of direct human community by a technological oligarchy that is understood to threaten life on the planet itself. The Unabomber expresses what is sometimes called an anti-tech/anti-civ (anti-technology and anti-civilizational) approach which opposes all manifestations of advanced technology rather than the specific mode of production associated with capitalism and capitalist uses of technology.

In this the association, already emerging as part of popular lore in the internet age, of the anarchist as Luddite found rather strong, and easy, expression. This earlier version of the anarchist as techno-primitive (or "future primitive" to use John Zerzan's phrase) or latter day Luddite machine smasher provided the main popular image of anarchists in the early years of online development. This image would also allow for, and encourage, a replaying of the popular mythology of the anarchist as primitive rebel—the enraged opponent of progress who, lacking other means, turns to terrorist acts of propaganda of the deed to smash the machines (or the megamachine of technological civilization) or blow up the edifice of industry (and its technologically meditated social relations).

The construction of the Unabomber as anarchist is, however, entirely ideological. The Unabomber, in his lengthy manifesto, actually reserves most of his condemnation for progressive groups, movements, and perspectives associated with anarchism or with which anarchists have lent support. These include leftism broadly, socialism, labor, feminist and gay and lesbian movements and animal rights.

At the same time, and perhaps more underground (or undernet), actual anarchists of a more collectivist or commu-nalist orientation were developing networks in the web. These early hackers, technophiles, designers, online organizers, and programmers were exploring convergences of anarchism with the (pre)internet. For these online anarchists the emergent web (which they were instrumental if unacknowledged in devel-oping) shared much in common with longstanding features of anarchism: decentralized, horizontal, participatory, democratic, and based in do it yourself (DIY) production and gift exchange. These anarchists saw themselves as web workers—as a new wave of artisanal producers, much like the watchmakers of Jura who provided an early impetus for anarchist communism in the 1800s.

The anarchists viewed the net as a means of self-production and self-determination (in labor as much as in anything). The main threats, in their view, were the state (and regulation and surveillance) and capital (and enclosure and privatization)—the dominant forces of political economy in capitalist societies. These were the twin forces that had always provided the social opposition for anarchists.

A Note on "Terrorism"

The term terrorism is a politically volatile, even slippery one. As philosopher Alain Badiou suggests: "It has no neutral currency" (2011, 19). Terrorism initially referred to a certain exercise of *state* power (leveled against targets designated as opponents of the state). The term has come, over time, to signify precisely the opposite—the actions of *non-state actors* who oppose a prevailing order. Those who maintain that order designate opposition as unacceptable—as terroristic (Badiou 2011, 18). All that remains the same is the targeting by states of non-state opponents, real or imagined. No longer is any distinction made between civilian and state victims of violence.

How can the acts of 9/11 be connected to the assassinations of the 1900s? How can those attacks be rendered the same as the events of 9/11. Clearly the current attempts to link individual acts of violence targeting state figures (in the nineteenth century) with the mass violence of 9/11 are performing an act of contortion. The term "terrorism" is, as Alain Badiou suggests "an intrinsically propagandistic term" (2011, 19).

On the whole we might conclude with Badiou: "It is clear that 'terrorism' is a non-existent substance, an empty name. But this void is precious since it can be filled" (2011, 20). None have been more proficient at filling it that the imperial powers (especially the US, Britain, and Canada) and the corporate mass media who mimic them in the West.

It might be said, too, that the term "war" has similarly lost meaning in the context of the post-9/11 world. Only now has it been possible to declare *war* on terrorism. For Badiou: "Indeed, how can war be declared on a few delinquent civilians, on some fanatical bombers, or on a group of anarchists" (2011, 26–27).

Repression, as Shantz (2012) has outlined, has been a constant response, to be sure, but it has taken the form of the police, not the military in acts of war.

In the end, contemporary actions of the anarchists, in the web and in the streets, are always affirmative. They assert their aims and take responsibility. There is no silence as followed the 9/11 attacks. As Badiou suggests, "with affirmative liberating, non-nihilistic political violence, responsibility is not only always claimed, but finds its essence in being claimed" (2011, 32–33). They always claim their acts as they claim themselves.

A Creative Passion

The Unabomber episode served to reinforce prejudices against anarchism that view anarchists as modern day Luddites hell bent on violently smashing any and all new technologies.

More than this, it positioned anarchism as a purely destructive, rather than critical or creative, force for change. Even as hacktivists became renowned for their tech skills and creative use of resources there would remain a sense that their main aim was not to build up but to tear down.

On one hand, any movement that seeks a radical (i.e. one that gets to the roots of social problems) change in social structures (and the abolition of specific systems, institutions, or tools of oppression or repression) will be susceptible to charges that they are destructive—which in a literal, if limited, sense, they are. A movement like anarchism, which explicitly seeks to end all systemic forms of exploitative authority are perhaps especially likely to be subjected to such claims and vulnerable to having such accusations stick.

The early anarchist theorist Mikhail Bakunin famously claimed that, "The passion for destruction is also a creative passion." By this is implied rather straightforwardly that the vision of the social critic or activist seeks a remaking of social relations. As a sculptor must often rework an earlier piece, taking apart the unsatisfactory aspects to build it up again, so too the social critic seeks not the end of society but a reworking, a remolding, of social life—to create something new, hopefully better.

The early twentieth century Red Scare saw a range of laws enacted that criminalized anarchist organizing—and indeed criminalized working class organizing that simply exhibited traits of anarchism in workplaces, such as direct action, wildcat strikes, sabotage, demands for workers' control, and certain forms of union organizing. The so-called criminal anarchism or criminal syndicalism laws served to break up working class radical organizations and drive anarchism underground. As notes, one result was that anarchism became a largely cultural, or subcultural, movement with its influences largely in such modernist artistic circles as dada, surrealism, fluxus, and post-figurative or post-representational art.

The reference to "criminal anarchism" did not die as the anarchist movements subsided. Indeed, in 2013 popular authors as well as academics have revived the notion of criminal anarchism to explain current forms of political violence and acts of terrorism. In one prominent article in the otherwise liberal *Huffington Post*, commentator Steven Kurlander uses the term criminal anarchism in reference to the Boston Marathon bombings—this despite the fact that the presumed bombers had no connection at all to anarchist movements, politics, or philosophies. In fact there is no sign of any kind that they even knew what anarchism, as either movement or theory, is.

Such is the mythic character of anarchism in the popular eye (or at least the mainstream media and academic eyes) that it can be deployed as a floating signifier for almost any extreme act—regardless of the reality of the act or those carrying out the act. Such is true, regardless, too, of the real world history of anarchist movements over almost two centuries.

One might do well to remember that the anarchists targeted in the various red scares and anti-terror panics have been largely labor activists and were not involved in violent, much less terrorist acts. If anything the modern hacktivists, techtivists, and cyber anarchists represent aspects of a long lineage of self-management and workers' control of industry—of anarchists motivated by attempts to self-manage their labors and use their technical skills to produce use values for communities rather than exchange values for capital.

Rather than trying to "blow up" the internet, or any other part of advanced technological society (a silly proposition anyway) most anarchists (whether technologically inclined or not) have viewed the internet and personal computer networks more broadly as potentially valuable self-organizing tools. As the activists of from TAO Communications to Riseup.net have argued, the real crimes are ones of control of technology and the purposes to which it is put—as a technological commons for human and ecological need or a privatized tech market for profit). Underlying these issues are the central ones of ownership and control. These are at the heart of the debates and efforts discussed in this book.

Still, despite this reality, the moral panic over hacktivists and cyber anarchists has been powerful (and potently deployed by states and corporations seeking to enclose the global techno-logical commons while criminalizing those who would mobilize opposition). Even more, it draws fundamentally upon tried and true tropes deployed against anarchists historically in the various anti-anarchist panics and scares since the late 1800s. To understand manifestations of contemporary power it is worth examining the current forms of these portrayals in some detail and this is undertaken in a subsequent chapter of *Cyber Disobedience*.

Chapter 2

Finding the Middle Ground in Cyberspace: A Content Analysis of Hackers in Film

Hackers have become an influential global community, affecting systems both inside and outside of cyberspace. This study was designed to explore the portrayal of hackers through five popular hacker films: "WarGames" (1983); "Sneakers" (1992); "Hackers" (1995); "Swordfish" (2001) and "V for Vendetta" (2005). Understanding the portrayal of hackers through content analysis is important to contemporary society with the insurgence of the loosely associated hacktivist group, "Anonymous." The data in the study was supported using a select review of pertinent academic journals and news articles. Moreover, insurrectionary anarchist theory was applied to the study in order to contextualize hackers as they have evolved throughout history. This study found that portrayals of hackers can be discerned into nine categories, with the three most popular being: revolutionary & political—shaping the world; advanced understanding of computers; and terrorist—anarchist enemy of the state. The data revealed that these portrayals were most prevalent and that a number of real world examples confirm the findings.

Ideas shape society. Some ideas are highly contagious and resilient spreading from person to person, like a virus. Meanwhile others pass us by comparatively without notice. Disseminating a popular idea rests upon systems of delivery and the capacity to resonate with many persons. Conceptually, this is a complex process. Twenty-first century ideas about hacking have largely been viewed with ambivalence and misconstrued trepidation. To some extent, society has a general sense of what hacking is and how hackers are delineated. Notwithstanding, it is important that the phenomenon is examined as society moves forward in the age of information and as the conspicuous hacktivist collective Anonymous comes to light. The idea of anonymity is not new and its inception is likely indeterminable. Until the age of information, knowledge was neither readily accessible nor could it be organized without significant time or expense. Today, the Internet has allowed ideas to be shared across the globe through a virtual medium consequently revolutionizing the way we think and live. To date, hackers have paved the way for Internet users to access a variety of applications ranging from corporate use to personal communications. Anonymous, a loosely associated hacktivist group has emerged over the last decade and strives to be the chaotic non-partisan group, only by the idea that information and knowledge should be free. Going forward into the technological age, there is a need to learn what has been mistakenly discerned hitherto as a haphazard collection of hacking.

When looking at hacker categories, we can discern three principal types: white-hats, black-hats, and grey-hats. A white-hat hacker is generally regarded as an ethical person who discovers weaknesses in a working security system and brings the attention to a network administrator (Wing 1998, 31). This type of hacker is useful for improving security systems and lessening opportunity for cyber-attacks. A black-hat is someone who "violates computer security for little reason beyond maliciousness or for personal gain" (Moore 2005, 258). Black-hats are generally regarded as criminal in contemporary society and have been associated with the malicious security hacks of the faceless hacktivist group, "Anonymous." The use in terminology for the above hacker types originates from Old Western films where the 'bad guys' wore black hats and the 'good guys' wore white ones (Neumann 2004, 132). Last but not least, there are grey-hats: a combination of a black-hat and white-hat hacker. This type of hacker is known to victimize those who are in opposition to their own sense of morality, and at the same time providing support to those whom they feel empathetic toward. Needless to say, hackers and hacking ought not to have been reduced to a binary summation.

The earliest examples of hacking took place in tandem with the first electronic computers. One of the world's first hackers, Nevil Maskelyne, was a 39-year-old British magician. The hack occurred in June of 1903 while physicist John Ambrose Fleming was preparing a demonstration to an eager audience at the Royal Institution's lecture theater in London, England. Fleming was demonstrating long-range wireless communication systems developed by his boss, Guglielmo Marconi. The aim was to showcase the first public transmission of Morse code over long distances, 300 miles away. Makelyne hacked into the system by beaming strong wireless pulses into the theater, and delivered a personal message: "There was a young fellow of Italy, who diddled the public quite prettily." The message was not well received. On the other hand, the hack highlighted the flaws in the technology's security network, and paved the way for improved technologies. In similar fashion, so-called "white-hat hackers" or "sneakers" explore such weaknesses today.

The activity of hacking is a misapprehended aspect of contemporary online society. Without fail, the idea of "hacking" generally pulls people in opposite directions. Is hacking an activity that is good or bad? Are hackers in cyberspace criminals or revolutionaries? In the computer world, a hacker has been described as someone who is committed to re-engineering computer systems and taking the technology of the computer into unexplored directions. In spite of this "hacking" does necessarily have to involve computers. More specifically, there is no generally agreed upon definition of what 'hacking' actually is. It's meaning is constantly being reinvented. In recent years, the media has mistakenly characterized the majority of hackers as being a threat to national security and to digital information systems (Gunkel 2005, 595). In any case, ideas around hacking should not be reduced to a binary summation. To complicate matters further, the Merriam-Webster Dictionary (2012) contains two contradictory entries for "a hacker": "a person who is inexperienced or unskilled at a particular activity" and "an expert at programming and solving problems with a computer." The fact of the matter is, hacking and hackers take on all sorts of shapes. Needless to say, the summation of who a hacker is or what constitutes hacking is far from conclusion as time passes and as knowledge continues apace.

In the following, we intend to present the various ways that hackers are portrayed in culture through contemporary film. This is accomplished through a content analysis approach that examines the depiction of hackers from the perspective of five Hollywood films: "WarGames" (1983), "Sneakers" (1992), "Hackers" (1995), "Swordfish" (2001), and "V for Vendetta" (2005). Guiding research questions took the following shape: how might hacking practices be a vehicle for individual or collective gain? How are they portrayed in film? Do film portrayals reflect cultural realities of hackers accordingly?

Method

Qualitative researchers have a number of methods at their disposal. The diversity in methods allows researchers to present evidence in a variety of sorts, and depending on approach, results may vary. Previous studies have looked at how hackers view themselves within their culture context (Jordan & Taylor 1998; Lakhani & Wolf 2003; Turgeman-Goldschmidt 2008) and others on how they are viewed by the general public (Taylor 1999; Warren 2003; Olsen 2012), but few studies have focused on how hackers are portrayed using content analysis and film. In order to guide decisions and give direction to our research, a deductive approach using anarchist theory to contextualize hackers in contemporary society was employed. Given that some hackers are apart of an underground community, and often mistakenly characterized as "criminal" or "deviant," the anarchist perspective fits well for the chosen films as themes of disorder, revolution, and lawlessness surfaced. Ultimately, the application of theory served as a map from where we could start and where we could go (McCotter 2001, 3).

The chosen method to contextualize the research was through content analysis. Content analysis is a method used in both qualitative and quantitative research and is described as "the study of recorded human communications, such as books, websites, paintings and laws" (Babbie 2003). The method was systematic yet flexible in its approach to coding as it allowed for concepts and themes that were not anticipated to emerge. The research was mostly exploratory, as it involved tapping into hidden aspects of social realities, hacking, but also previous knowledge on the topic enabled educated analysis. When it comes to sampling procedure, we chose to use a combination of purposive and theoretical sampling. In terms of purposive sampling, the sources for our data were chosen based on our research questions and available resources. The use of film as a data source was unobtrusive and non-interactive, preventing timely and stringent ethical guidelines compulsory with human participants.

One of the most pivotal steps to gathering data on this community was deciding on the samples. Initially, a number of movies came to mind when we thought of the topic, but we wanted to ensure that each film presented offered a distinct asset to the product. To help set parameters to the sample, "Top 20 movies about computer hacking" was entered into Google's search engine. Consequently, five Hollywood films were chosen based on hacking or hackers as the aforementioned theme. The interpretation of these films rested upon the assumption that "we can learn about our society by investigating the material items produced within it" (Hesse-Biber & Leavy 2011, 227). This small sample allowed for rich and thick descriptions to contextualize contemporary hackers. During the research process, two goals were kept in mind: discover relevant categories for hackers' portrayals and examine the shared or contested relationships among them. There were two primary benefits of using film as a sample as Reinharz (1992) explains: (1) the data are non-interactive, and (2) the data exist independent of the researcher (as cited in Hesse-Biber & Leavy 2011, 228). Another strength of the data is seen its ability to offer symbolic representations and includes some measure of diversity among each film. Though, it should be understood that the film producers fictionalize facts that deviate from real-life situations of hackers, but may not be realistic portrayals. In terms of the research, reliability and validity would have been increased had there been more time to employ triangulation methods (i.e., combining more than one qualitative or quantitative method). Regardless, the film and literature review allowed the research to be more advantaged than disadvantaged in the process. If time constraints were not an issue, we would have conducted interviews with hackers in the community. Also, we would have applied two different theoretical perspectives (an anarchist approach and a strain theory approach) to investigate the phenomenon. In particular Robert Agnew's (1992) contemporary strain theory would have been applied by looking at expectations and actual achievements of hackers in society, and how blocked opportunities results in personal disappointment and how this may serve as a motivational factor. From the outset of the research, this theory came to mind as we consider blocked opportunity to play a key role in the individual variation found within the hacker community.

Data for the study were derived from five Hollywood films between the years of 1983-2005. The use of Hollywood films was based out of the feasibility of access and low cost to rent. The starting point of 1983 corresponded with the first film, "WarGames," by Lawrence Lasker. This film was important for establishing a starting point as it introduced hacking to the wider public in a period where the usage of computers was on the rise.

The next film we chose was "Sneakers" (1992) by Phil Alden Robinson as it presents the ethical "white-hat hacker" to the audience and revealed the importance of network security. The third film was "Hackers" (1995) by Iain Softley, which presents "black-hats" and "white-hats" pitted against one another in a corporate extortion conspiracy case with capabilities to hack and manipulate physical systems. Next, Dominic Sena's "Swordfish" (2001) demonstrated the virtuosity of hackers and the lengths that some are willing to take for money and love, concurrently revealing themes of anarchy and lawlessness. Lastly, "V for Vendetta" (2005) by James McTeigue presented a theoretical basis to hacking and contextualizes present-day hacking efforts by the faceless hacktivist group "Anonymous." The ending point for the films was effortlessly decided as no film has had a greater influence—both symbolically (e.g., with the use of Guy Fawkes masks displaying both affiliation and ensuring anonymity) and philosophically (e.g., one of vigilante justice and natural law)—on Anonymous.

Qualitative research is a situated activity where the observer focuses and interprets the world around them. At the heart of the research, audiences are better able to understand the researchers position in society and how they observe others in their daily lives based on their interpretations. When it came to the research process, there were initial assumptions relating to the depiction of hackers. Particular biases that we brought to our research in regards to hacking, whether criminal or non-malicious, are similar to those seen by grey hat hackers. Based on our personal values, attitudes, and beliefs, hacking and hackers are seen as either ethical or non-ethical. For example, if a hacker were financially motivated then we viewed that person as harmful to society as we feel that hacking should be selfless and that it should be conducive to creating something for public use. When hackers strive for revolutionary or political aims, generally we held a favourable view toward their goals as the films idealized propositions that we cheerfully assent to. The process of hacking without permission, to us, appears normalized with technology at societies disposal one way or another and where access to information seems requisite. At any given moment the digital brain—*that is the Internet*—provides users with a wealth of knowledge. With the aid of hackers, private information and knowledge can be exposed to those who follow and those who listen. It is plausible that this phenomenon deters individual and corporate rights to privacy, although hacks by Anonymous can sometimes stem from a vision to expose the harm that others are doing. Needless to say, the position that one takes against hackers will be highly reliant on their perspective of the act and whether or not they are being victimized in the process. It is one thing to believe that it is "good" or "bad" and it is entirely another to be hacked and victimized as a result. Notwithstanding, hacking is a multifaceted phenomenon that can be of value in the political affairs of life.

Another essential step to conducting proper research is ethical dilemmas. In this case, research was based on a content analysis of audiovisual material. The ethical issues in this process were not directly related to the collecting and coding of data. Gathering the films involved legal transactions and did not require permission of use given that it is publically available. Ethical dilemmas were more critical to the nature of hacking alone and dependent on an individual's position, whether hacking is ethical or not. For example, hackers in the films and, in reality, are sometimes depicted as being "deviant." This gives rise to the question of who determines deviant behaviour? If we are to take a legal approach, then the answer is more clear and explicit. Nevertheless, if our ethical position is driven by culture then the question becomes relative vis-à-vis how people conceptualize issues around hacking and hackers. In any case, ethics were not as important in this process as there were no controls that could have been taken to control how the creators in the films portray hackers.

Hacker Portrayals

The coding process in this study generated nine categories revealing the various ways in which hackers are portrayed through film. Initial literal codes yielded eighteen distinct categories but the coding process became more specific as the data was interpreted and as relationships were drawn out. Our aim was to obtain different movie plots to observe how hackers were portrayed and where variety exists among the community. With this goal in mind, we were able to compare and contrast hackers across the board. Once the films were chosen, equal time was allotted to each movie, thus ensuring equal observation, sufficient coding time, and preventing potential favoritism. Data was then collected over a five-day period and each of the films was analyzed in chronological order. This process averaged about two minutes of coding per every one minute of film.

In this following sections, we present the dominant portrayals of hackers through the use of content analysis in descending order from most frequent to least frequent: (a) revolutionary & political—shaping the world; (b) advanced understanding of computers; (c) terrorist—anarchist enemy of the state; (d) fun and entertainment seeking; (e) malicious, harmful intensions and fearless of punishment; (f) curiosity; (g) lack of malicious intensions; (h) financially motivated; and, (i) vengeful.

Revolutionary & Political – Shaping the World

The revolutionary and political hacker was the most recurrent depiction. In relation to computing, hackers of the early twentieth century shaped our contemporary society, owing to the fact that some were more eager than others in bringing their ideas to fruition. Revolutions that hackers undergo throughout these films shapes society and change the course of history in online and offline communities, real and fictional. The film "V for Vendetta" (2005) by James McTeigue is a contemporary film where Libertarians and Anarchists take up revolution against oppressive governments. In this film, a totalitarian regime, reflecting a Nazi-like propagandist state, governs the United Kingdom. With personal liberties infringed upon through the course of censorship, curfew, and substantial cultural material being blacklisted from use, society prepares for a coming insurrection. The protagonist of the film "V" is fed up with the government inflicting hardship and constraint within the community and takes up arms against state. "V" begins as a nonviolent demonstrator who believes, "words will always retain their power. Words are the means to meaning for those who will listen; the enunciation of truth." This demonstrates that he is pensive and searches for an audience to follow him in a time where the masses are apprehensive to tread against powers that be. "People should not be afraid of their governments, governments should be afraid of their people," he argues. He suggests that the public has accepted subordination and that collectively they could forcibly overthrow government. This quote aligns with Slevin's (2003) Anarchist philosophy as "V" holds the state to be immoral and hopes to restore the nation to a utopian form. Ultimately, "V" destroys the Old Bailey, the central criminal court in the city of London, to remind the country of what it has forgotten. He explains that "cruelty, injustice, intolerance and depression" have come to be the norm and that nearly "400 years ago a great citizen [Guy Fawkes] wished to embedded the 5th of November forever in our memory. His hope was to remind the world that fairness, justice, and freedom are all more than words; they are perspectives." This statement is relevant to contemporary society with the group Anonymous, as members fight against oppressive regimes in Egypt, Syria, and the United States (Schwartz 2012a). The later section of that quote makes a fundamental point of how hackers are portrayed: it's a matter of "perspective." This idea is essential to how the opponents of "V" view his stratagem. From their point of view, he is an anarchist and a terrorist who is fearless of punishment and a stern opponent to the role that the state wishes he would assume, which may be passivity or conformity. However, he firmly believes that "this country needs more than a building right now, it needs hope," and is unperturbed by the repercussions of his actions as they are selfless in his mind. Some under the banner of Anonymous assume a similar analogy in their fight for freedom of speech online and offline. More importantly, the film provided the so-called face to the faceless collective with the adoption of the Guy Fawkes masks, unifying affiliation and commitment to their shared cause while also serving to protect individual identity (Waites 2011). We would also argue that the use of Guy Fawkes masks by Anonymous hints at the removal of hierarchy within the collectives' structure as "members" openly declare opposition to authority, believing that the current state of affairs is undesirable.

In the film in "Swordfish" (2001) by Dominic Sena, the revolutionary and political hacker is presented in the back-story of protagonist Gabriel Shear (John Travolta). Shear argues his political beliefs forthright, believing that "some men are put here to shape destiny, to protect freedom, despite the atrocities they must commit. I am one of those men." This quote reveals that the means to an end are not always virtuous but necessary. While "V" believes "violence can be used for good; justice," Shear's thinks he is "at war with anyone who infringes on America's freedom." The two, however, differ substantially as Gabriel possesses alternative motives, be it financial. In Iain Softley's "Hackers" (1995), the creator suggests that hackers "exist[s] without nationality, skin colour, or religious bias." In reality, this statement is not true as members of Anonymous openly declare their disgust in the Church of Scientology (Dodd 2011), and more recently the Westboro Baptist Church (Stryker, 2011). The quote reveals that hackers are essentially stateless suggesting concepts of society related to anarchist perspectives (Taylor 1982, 6). By taking an anarchist perspective, the excerpt aligns with Merriam-

Webster's (2011) definition of anarchy: "a state of lawless or political disorder due to the absence of governmental authority." In the context of the film, it is plausible that some hackers believe that a utopian society is one in which individuals enjoy complete freedom without government; as well, certain institutions and systems that are seen as oppressive (like the Church of Scientology and the Westboro Baptist Church who are both engaged in controversial issues).

Advanced Understanding of Computers

For hackers, computer skillfulness is essential to their ability to communicate their message as they have a plethora of technological delivery systems at their disposal. In "Swordfish" (2001), Gabriel Shear (John Travolta) exclaims to Stanley Jobson (Hugh Jackman), "with a laptop and a phone line you can make God look like a thirteen-year-old with a stack of Playboys and lack of imagination", suggesting that he is a technological geniuses with remarkably skillful. The comical excerpt gives an enormous amount of credit to hackers with the use of language and implies that skilled hackers are akin to a Supreme Being. In contrast, enemies and opponents of hackers do not describe them with the same positive remarks and rather discredit their work to being "no different than any other terrorist." In Lawrence Lasker's "WarGames" (1983), computer skillfulness is put to its limits when protagonist David Lightman (Mathew Broderick) accidently accesses a United States military supercomputer—the War Operation Plan Response (WOPR)—capable of causing nuclear war and starting World War III. In the film, hacker David Lightman begins by engaging in phreaking, an activity that garners unpermitted access to telecommunication technology. With his skillful tactic, he is able to "call every number in California for free." In the midst of this process, Lightman gains entry to the WOPR and accidently runs a program nearly causing a nuclear war between Soviet Russia and the United

States. Ironically, the film portrays the hacker as being extremely virtuous, however, he uses a Macintosh computer in the film that was not capable of hacking at the time. Furthermore, Apple computers are rarely used today for hacking purposes since they are not part of the open-source software. Lastly, in the film "Hackers" (1995), the computer hackers are described as being like a "samurai," a "keyboard cowboy," as well as warriors thus implying power and determination in their dexterity in the use of computers. Although the films are fictional in their depiction of their skills, it is no surprise that real life hackers perform with considerable virtuosity as they navigate throughout the techno-logical landscape.

Terrorist–Anarchist Enemy of the State

A common theme present at the forefront of the data was terrorism. Likewise, a hacktivist is both a hacker and an activist who utilizes hacking to promote social or political cause. The parallels between the two are similar in the sense of having an awareness and action related to their ideologically driven beliefs. The difference in the use of language—whether described as "hacktivists" or "terrorists"—most likely has to do with a matter of perspective and whether someone has a favorable or unfavorable view. To some, their actions may be seen as heroic and noble, whereas others will see the person's attempts as acts of treason and anarchistic. When "V" in "V for Vendetta" destroyed the Old Bailey, High Chancellor Adam Sutler (John Hurt) exclaims, "I want this terrorist found, and I want him to under-stand what terror really means." This character in this example explicitly mentions his perspective of the hacker. Ironically, he reveals that state acts of terrorism are acceptable. Sutler even goes so far as say that V is a "psychotic terrorist" and that they "can't except him to act like [them]," revealing that hackers do not fit within the supposed functionality of society. In "Swordfish" Jobson describes Shear as "no different than any other terrorist," implying that although a hacker may view himself or herself as a revolutionary, a political activist or a hacktivist, its adversaries rarely characterize them from this perspective.

Malicious, Harmful Intentions and Fearless of Punishment

The fourth most popular portrayal of hackers in film is that they are malicious, have harmful intensions, and are fearless of punishment. In the film "V for Vendetta" examples of this portrayal are seen within the opening scenes when V destroys the Old Bailey. The act is committed intentionally to "remind the country of what it has forgotten." Terrorism is intentionally used to convey his message to the public and seemingly carries forth his agenda without fear of punishment. In "WarGames" (1983) Lightman, and intelligent and thoughtful hacker, explains, "you can only go to jail if you're over 18." The protagonist throughout the film unintentionally engages in harmful acts of hacking, however, his lack of *mens rea* does not discount the harmful and malicious nature of the act. In reality, this theme resonates among many members of Anonymous as some are unafraid of persecution as they believe what they are doing is necessary for the benefit of us all (Gallagher 2012). Moreover, many hackers engage in illegal activities that, to some, may be seen as moral and just. For example, operations under the banner of Anonymous have targeted Jihadist websites, pedophiles, and child pornography as they realize that police agencies take years and have to follow legal process along the way (Mlot 2012). Subsequently, some hackers are doing police work without fear of repercussion because many in society might agree that their aims are virtuous, thus not persecuting their actions.

Fun and Entertainment Seeking

This category was the most surprising in the research in terms of the lack of examples where hackers are engaging in fun or enter-tainment seeking. It was not anticipated that there would only be a handful of examples in light of Orly Turgeman-Goldschmidt's (2005) article "Hackers' Accounts: Hacking as a Social Entertainment." In her study, the researcher was able to form ten categories of accounts used by hacker to "justify the wide range of computer offences they commit in software piracy, hacking, and phreaking" (12). The most notable account given was "fun, thrill, and excitement", which provided a comprehensive understanding of the hacking phenomenon as hackers offer society new rules for play: a form of entertainment. Nevertheless, this theme did not reveal itself as often in the research process. It was anticipated that this would be the most popular portrayal given that powerful hacking collectives, like Anonymous, begun with simple pranks on 4chan—the imageboard site where the collective originated in 2003—and later engaging in hacking simply "for the lulz" (Williams 2011). In fact, the group was not renowned for widespread hacktivism until much later in 2008 with "Project Chanology." The operation was a protest against the Church of Scientology who attempted to censor an internal video of Tom Cruise that had leaked onto YouTube. Subsequently, Anonymous hacked and defaced the Church of Scientology's website and it was here where the world got a glimpse of their hacktivism and ominous signoff on blogs, websites, and elsewhere seen today exclaiming, "We are Anonymous. We are Legion. We do not forgive. We do not forget. Expect us" (Olson 2012, 4).

In the movie "Sneakers," the film opens with two hackers committing pranks and phreaking, ultimately leading one of the hackers to be apprehended by the FBI. In the final scenes of the film, the arrested hacker mistakenly believes that everything he was doing was for revolutionary and political purpose, whereas the other who was not arrested discredits him suggesting that "it wasn't a journey, it was a prank." This excerpt reveals that the matter of perspectives lies heavily in the eyes of the beholder. While one black-hat hacker believed that they should continue to engage in malicious hacks, the white-hat hacker wishes that it had never escalated past mere pranks. When Lightman is apprehended by the FBI in the film "WarGames," an agent asks him why he would set the WOPR to run a program potential causing World War III, to which one agent responds, "he does these sorts of things for fun." This demonstrates that his intentions were non-malicious and that his hacking motives solely were to play a game, and he unknowingly hacked into a powerful military computer.

Curiosity

Without doubt, hackers engage in various activities out of mere curiosity. In the article "Hackers as Tricksters of the Digital Age: Creativity in Hacking Culture," author Svetlana Nikitina (2012) presents an examination of hacking as it relates to American popular culture and service economy. In this article, Nikitina portrays hackers as being a "universal changeling" (2012, 136), a person who subverts clearly established hierarchies and crosses all boundaries as a matter of course. In order to illustrate her findings, the author makes parallels between hackers and trickster gods in myths. The reason for this connection is that both hackers and tricksters offer a perspective on divinity that combines goodness and wickedness (Nikitina 2012, 135). In the study, the author presents four categories for comparison for a hacker-trickster: the motif of duplicity (propensity for lying and deceit), the motif of boundary crossing (propensity for long-distance travel and connection making), the motif of subversion of power (propensity for pranks and deconstruction of power hierarchies), and the motif of creativity and craftsmanship (propensity for finding creative solutions and making original discoveries) (Nikitina 2012, 136). In summary, Nikitina presents hackers as having an "addiction to knowledge, love of technology, and boundary-crossing for its own sake" (2012, 146), suggesting that hackers are curious by nature.

In the film "Swordfish," Gabriel Shear's curiosity leads him to wonder "what countries will harbor terrorists, when they realize the consequences of what I will do?" This excerpt reveals willingness to create social experiments for the purpose of envisioning what the future may bear. Another example can be found in film "Hackers" when one hacker is talking to a police officer and claims that "yes, I am a criminal. My crime is that of curiosity." These examples suggest that hackers are willing to go to extreme lengths to have their ideas come to fruition, while simultaneously remaining fearless of persecution or to pursue their curiosity and enter into highly secure systems. In the real world, many in the hacker community share this message as hacks are often done because they powered by curiosity (Nikitina 2012, 149).

Lack of Malicious Intentions

For hackers in the aforementioned films, the majority of their aims do not result from malicious intentions. In the film "WarGames," David Lightman did not have malicious intentions when he accidently hacked into NORAD's War Operation Plan Response computer. Lightman accessed the system by accident and without knowledge that the program was not a game he said, "let's play thermonuclear war." This excerpt demonstrates the innocence that the character possessed and in reality he was only seeking fun and entertainment. In "Sneakers," we observe similar 'innocent' acts when one hacker honorably explains, "I simply want peace on earth and good will to good men." This suggests that the hacker had no intention of causing harm to any persons and that the white-hat hacking that he engages in throughout the film is done, from his perspective, for mutual benefit to the general population. This category, however, would least likely be portrayed in reality, as news consortiums rarely would produce articles on hacking that lack malicious or harmful intent (Gunkel 2005, 595).

Financially Motivated

For most hackers, the least likely motivator is money. This category is similar to the findings by Orly Turgeman-Goldschmidt (2005) where only one of her fifty-four Israeli hackers' accounts in her study revealed money to be a motivation for hacking (14). In the film "Swordfish," money was a main motivator for Stanley Jobson at the beginning of the film when he is offered, "$100,000 just to meet [Gabriel Shear]." As the movie progresses, Jobson's motivation increases exponentially when he accepts a job for ten million dollars to hack into banking system to steal nearly ten billion dollars for Shear, an insurrectionary anarchist. Similarly, hacker Martin Brice (Robert Redford) in "Sneakers" accepts a job from the NSA to locate and retrieve a "black box"—a device with access to the Federal Reserve, the U.S. department of Emergency and the Air Traffic Control System—for the sum of $175,000 and a clean criminal record. If we are to apply this portrayal to reality, the topic is not equally recurrent. This example becomes less likely in reality when we look to examples of Anonymous such as "Operation Robin Hood" where hacktivists accessed thousands of private and government organization stealing their credit card information and making donations to charities on Christmas Eve (Williams 2011). So while money may not be a central motivation, it can play a part at times.

Vengeful

The least common portrayal of hackers is that they are vengeful. As Turgeman-Goldschmidt (2005) argues, "revenge is an emotional factor that is not related to computer characteristics offences" (17). In "Swordfish," Shear reveals his vengefulness and explains, "If they bomb a church, we bomb ten. They hijack a plane, we take out an airport." This example proposes that some hackers are forceful by nature and are in need of having the upper hand. Themes of revenge are also manifested in the film

"V for Vendetta." Apart from the explicitly vindictive title, the philosophy of V was one of vigilante justice, annihilation, and also one of creation. The protagonist sought to avenge the harm that was done to him with an eye for an eye, a tooth for a tooth mentality. Needless to say, his vengeful behaviour emanated from intentions that would create a better society for the people of England. In the film, V felt as though he was a prisoner to the government, even while living as a so-called free man. His beliefs, however, seem rightly justified as the government conducted horrific experiments on him while in he was a prisoner at Larkhill (details in Appendix E). His revengeful nature is also reflected in his favorite film, "The Count of Monte Cristo." Identical to the plot of *Monte Cristo*, V is wrongfully imprisoned, escapes jail, and is determined to getting his revenge. Interestingly, a brief clip of "The Count of Monte Cristo" appears in the film "Hackers" (1995) when character Dade Murphy seeks revenge against hacker "Acid Burn" for hacking into his computer. The symbolism in both films suggests that hackers are vengeful and carry vendettas across time while also viewing themselves as heroic or trope figures.

Each hacker is unique. Portrayal of hackers are neither exclusively agreed upon nor easily summed up in one sentence. It is a matter of perspective. And our subjective perspectives change everything. Members of the hacking community take special precautions against being caught. It is for this reason that portrayals differ as we shift in and out of our own socially constructed realities. Looking through the three most common portrayals of hackers—revolutionary and political, advanced understanding of computers, and terrorists—it is open to question whether or not hackers may well be the most powerful group shaping contemporary society. In any period of time, people invariably adapt to their perpetually changing environments as a survival strategy. Notwithstanding, life today is somewhat dualistic as we exist and connect both physically and virtually. With the Internet being an integral part of our daily lives in western democracies, it is conceivable that hackers will increase in numbers and that greater access to our personal data will be available. The irony of uploading our lives for the entire world to see is that it is largely done voluntarily. For this reason a person can decide to opt out of cyberspace, but this option is becoming less available as a quasi-dependent relationship between machines and humans continues apace.

Without a doubt, hackers and the collective Anonymous are a phenomenon worthy of attention. Whether you are a citizen, government employee, or policy maker; the world will have to decide how to deal with hackers as societies move forward in the information age. The answer, however, should not be criminalization or heavy punishment toward hackers as it has recently been observed. Hackers have much to offer society and we have much to learn from various communities. This project, without adornment, can serve as a one starting point for examining this community through the use of content analysis. Findings confirmed initial assumptions that the community is largely counter-cultural, works within a quasi-cyber-criminal framework, and are largely regarded as radical revolutionaries or terrorists, depending on one's perspective. In contemporary society, hackers are either portrayed as good or bad, with little movement in between. As one Anonymous hacker, Commander X, argues, "Anonymous is the art of indignation. Anonymous is the art of being one and yet being nothing. Anonymous is what happens when governments and corporations screw up too badly" (Solyom 2012). Without a doubt, some could argue that there are hackers in reality that explicitly fall into these categories; however, again, it is a matter of perspective.

As the project evolved, the data tested and challenged what we knew. With vast amounts of information on the issue, it took an enormous amount of time to decide which avenue would be most fitting given the timeframe. Overall, throughout the research process we clarified questions and meaning based upon initial assumptions. In a world dominated by technology, it seems likely that research on the subject matter of hacker's portrayals using film as content analysis is in its infancy given that few films to date that portray hackers' and their lives. The results of this study can be extrapolated for further research in the future. If our own research were to be expanded in the area, we would look at what social conditions produce ethical hackers and ethical hacking. Likewise, we would like to explore the socio-political or economic conditions that drive hackers to be law-abiding, deviant or civil disobedient. Throughout the research over the past year on Anonymous, it seems that blocked economic and social opportunity in today's society has driven some hackers to drift in-and-out of favorable and unfavorable views of the law. Without a doubt, hackers will not subside until a balance is struck between access to information, transparency and equality in society.

Chapter 3

Sailing the Cyber Sea: Hacktivism and a Capitalist Response to Piracy

Everyone agrees that the Age of Information is here. Already, the Internet has become a collective intelligence of digitized knowledge. Emerging from the collaboration and competition of capitalist systems, the global community strives to create preventative measures for securing the ubiquitous territory. The World Wide Web has allowed for an ongoing global exchange of ideas; however this is currently under threat. It's likely that 2011 will be remembered by future generations as the year of Distributed Denial of Service (DDoS) attacks.[1] There's nothing new about this kind of hacktivism[2], but its use has accelerated; and the attention has warranted mainstream publicity thanks to a faceless Internet hacking idea, respectfully named "Anonymous." The collective is loosely organized and its membership is open to any person willing to engage in Internet hacktivism given that they are not taking credit for their attacks (i.e., anonymously). One idea of anonymous is simple: freedom of speech and information. The name originated as an Internet meme through a virtual community on the popular imageboard website, 4chan, by members whose identities were unknown to one another. On the imageboard site, registration and names are not required. As a result, the only thing that matters is the ideas that foster in the nonhierarchical community. Philosophically, some parts of Anonymous work on a system of anarchy as they strive to push toward a society that is free oppression and corruption. The loose-knit collective bestows several agendas, but there is no identifiable leader or goal. Simply put: their philosophy knows no boundaries as the Internet and the streets are their playgrounds. They are everywhere. And because Anonymous is an idea, it is unstoppable. Politically, some participants stand on left-wing practices and ideologies as they recognize and fight against the current capitalist-based society, and strive toward an egalitarian global community. Anonymous strives to be the chaotic neutral united by the idea that information and knowledge should be free.

The idea of anonymity is not new. And the starting point is likely indeterminable. Some argue that the Internet hacktivist group, Anonymous, may be traced philosophically to a specific piece of literature. A French essay entitled, *The Coming Insurrection*, has become the "manifesto" for some as the essay hypothesizes the "imminent collapse of capitalist culture" (2009, n.p.).[3] The essay was written by an anonymous group of contributors who call themselves the "Invisible Committee." The book is divided into two parts: the first presents a diagnosis, similar to the Communist Manifesto, of the current capitalist structure. The latter part illustrates how to effectively mobilize to potentially produce an anti-capitalist revolution through political, social, and environmental means. In the first part of the book, the authors are effective in illustrating some of the current social crises in terms of structural organizations as they advocate for a communal approach:

> Organizations are obstacles to organizing ourselves. In truth, there is no gap between what we are, what we do, and what we are becoming. Organizations—political or labor, fascist or anarchist—always begin by separating, practically, these aspects of existence. It's then easy for them to present their idiotic formalism as the sole remedy to this separation. To organize is not to give structure to weakness. It is above all to form bonds—bonds that are by no means neutral—terrible bonds. The degree of organization is measured by the intensity of sharing—material and spiritual. (15)

Comparable to the *Manifesto of the Communist Party* by Karl Marx and Friedrich Engels, *The Coming Insurrection* outlines current social breakdowns in an emerging capital-based market.

Two centuries of capitalism and market nihilism have brought us to the most extreme alienation—from our selves, from others, from worlds. The fiction of the individual has decomposed at the speed that it was becoming real. Children of the metropolis, we offer this wager: that it's in the most profound deprivation of existence, perpetually stifled, perpetually conjured away, that the possibility of communism resides.[4]

The notion of alienation presented by the Invisible Committee is identified by "seven circles": self, social relations, work, the economy, urbanity, the environment, and to close civilization. The language of the text reflects a similar tone to Marx and Engels as they argue that communists should disdain to conceal their views, and "openly declare that their ends can be attained only by the forcible overthrow of all existing social conditions... the proletarians have nothing to lose but their chains. They have a world to win."[5] Interestingly, The Invisible Committee cautions about the use of the using the word "communism" as the word is no longer considered very fashionable and has incessantly been tattered through propaganda to identify hostile enemies. In short, *The Coming Insurrection* calls for all power to be in the hands of communes and that society is currently situated within the collapse of a civilization; it is within this reality that we must choose sides. And many have.

By tracing back to the origins of the word "Hacktivism," and the means in which hacktivists planned on achieving their political ends, we can see an ideological dichotomy. The word "hacktivism" was coined in 1996 by Omega (Oxblood Ruffin 2004, n.p.)—a member of the Cult of the Dead Cow (cDc): a computer hacker organization. He linked the word to Article 19 of the United Nations Declaration of Human Rights (UNDHR), which read "Everyone has the right to freedom of opinion and expression; this right includes freedom to hold opinions without interference and to seek, receive and impart information and ideas through any media and regardless of frontiers." The idea for Omega was simple: connecting technology and human rights. At this point in time, Omega was in contact with the Legal Director of the Electronic Frontier Foundation (EFF), Cindy Cohn, who explained that the UNDHR was a declaration and not legally binding. Article 19 of the International Covenant on Civil and Political Rights (ICCPR)—another United Nations document—essentially said that same thing, "everyone shall have the right to freedom and expression; this right shall include freedom to seek, receive and impart information and ideas of all kinds, regardless of frontiers, either orally, in writing or in print, in the form of art, or through any other media of his choice." Omega understood that hacking for human right was one thing, but there had to be established and clear rules for engagement on how their political ends should be achieved. He also knew that it did not take a lot of people to make change, but rather that it took one good programmer. But a separation occurred along the way. Some members wanted to engage in illegal activities of hacktivism by using Denial of Service (DoS) attacks, and to interfere with the process of economic exchange. Meanwhile, others believed that the means to an end should be guided through established legal processes. In turn, the Internet would be lawfully utilized as a medium to transmit and to receive information in public forums. One goal for Omega was to circumvent government communication systems, rather than hacking. This ideological dichotomy set the stage for different "political hats" of conducting hacktivism, which can be seen in the present day with the online movement behind the idea of "Anonymous". Today, there are White-Hats, who engage in pro-security movements by finding weak points in online security and reporting it; Black-Hats, who engage in anti-security movement by finding weak points online and using it to their advantage; Grey-Hats, who engage in both anti-security and pro-security movements depending on their own views of a company or an industry; and finally those who do not wear a hat and simply observe and discuss the hacks. As a result of these different sentiments, there is a vast assortment of political ideologies and targets for these anonymous hacks. And because it is difficult for law enforcement agencies and governments to pinpoint the characterized offending activity, a multitude of responses have incurred, which in effect impact all users in cyberspace.

At the moment, members of Anonymous are sailing the stormy seas of cyberspace as they fight against piracy laws being imposed around the world in reaction to hacktivists. The cohesive philosophical essay—The Coming Insurrection—explains, "From now on, to materially organize for survival is to materially organize for attack." This statement assumes that people must fight for what they have in order to survive; there is nothing to lose. In the United States, two controversial bills are in play: Stop Online Piracy Act (SOPA) and Preventing Real Online Threats to Economic Creativity and Theft of Intellectual Property Act (PIPA). Stop Online Piracy Act was introduced as a means to expand U.S. law enforcement agencies ability to fight online piracy and copyright infringement of intellectual property. PIPA is a proposed law that would provide U.S. law enforcement agencies with more power to access websites dedicated to publishing "infringing or counterfeit goods,"[6] notably those who are beyond U.S. borders. The SOPA bill demonstrates the powerful extent of the U.S. government throughout several sections:

Section 102(a)(2) permits the attorney general to take action against foreign sites (i.e., sites that do not fall under U.S. jurisdiction) if "they owner or operator of such Internet site is facilitating the commission of [copyright infringement]

The currently in effect SOPA bill now allows the U.S. government to unilaterally censor foreign websites and makes it a felony to post a copyrighted song or video. Despite problems obvious problems with this bill (e.g., U.S. law enforcements ability to shut down foreign websites without a trial or conviction), the bill is extremely vague and many sites such as *YouTube* and *Facebook,* which hosts millions of users who post copyrighted songs and videos, are now at risk for prosecution. As a result, the vast majority of Internet users, especially among the youth who use social media and social entertainment networks sites (*YouTube, Twitter, Facebook)*, become criminalized and thus the censorship of the Internet sets sail. Undoubtedly, software piracy and intellectual property infringements are a crime. Despite this, it is problematic to allow U.S. law enforcement agencies to engage in Internet censorship. The Internet should be an open-source[7] platform as almost anything can be considered "knowledge" should be readily available and accessible; but if government agencies come in and are able to remove websites without trail or criminalize those beyond their continental borders, retaliation will ensue.[8] And it has.

One of the most notable coordinated responses was a website blackout that occurred on January 18th, 2012, with an estimated 7,000 other websites arranging a blackout in protest of the SOPA and PIPA bills. Notable participants in the SOPA/PIPA blackout included Wikipedia, who argued that if these two bills pass, it would be devastating to the free and open web. Wikipedia Foundation's Executive Director, Sue Gardner, stated: "Where it can be censored without due process, it hurts the speaker, the public, and Wikimedia. Where you can only speak if you have sufficient resources to fight legal challenges, or if your views are pre-approved by someone who does, the same narrow set of ideas already popular will continue to be all anyone has meaningful access to."[9] Once the mainstream media caught wind of the global fight, industries throughout the U.S. began to pick sides. On one side, open information websites like *Wikipedia* and *Reddit* stood against the proposed bills; the other side included industries such as *Recording Industry Association of America* (RIAA) and *Sony Electronics, Inc.* In a retaliatory effort, those who supported the proposed bills were subject to a string of attacks by Anonymous hacktivists[10] warning and demonstrating that the "online pirates" hold the power of the Internet and possess the knowledge to shut down websites, much like U.S. law enforcement. Although, unlike the police, Anonymous hacktivists deface websites and oftentimes post alternate replacement websites in order to relay messages to the public and the companies by directing threats to their economic capital. Even more troublesome for private industries, emails and personal account information are often released to the public. A problem that lies behind American governments is that if they decide that they are going to put breaks on the Internet, there will always be an alternate venue to by-pass domestic and foreign laws. Anonymous members illustrate that Internet security is largely an illusion, as it only takes one skilled computer programmer to be able to overcome a network. Furthermore, Internet users anonymity is also equally suscep-tible as hacktivists sometimes fail to take the necessary precau-tionary steps in order to protect their identity.

In 2011, Sony Entertainment, Inc. was supposedly hacked by a group of six members. The hacking led to 24.6 million Play Station Network users being shut out of service. Information that was obtained from the attack included 12,700 credit card numbers and expiration dates, email addresses and passwords, birth dates, gender, phone numbers, and 10,700 direct debit records for customers in Germany, Austria, Netherlands and Spain.[11] The attack on Sony also led to their network being down for over a month due to the companies attempt to restore and improve the network security. On March 6, 2012, Hector Xavier Monsegur (aka Sabu) was arrested as a "member" of Anonymous, Internet Feds, and LulzSec (a splinter group), and pleaded guilty on August 15, 2011. Sabu was arrested as the suspected ringleader of an offset from the group "Anonymous" and was sought after by the FBI for causing a reign of cyber-terror during the summer months of 2011; he hacked websites including the CIA, Sony, and several financial institutions including HBGary, inc. and HBGary Federal LLC. The hacking caused damages to these institutions estimated in millions of dollars around the globe. Sabu was extremely brilliant and always took precautions to hide is Internet protocol (I.P.) address through proxy services. Despite this, he made a critical mistake of not hiding it when he logged onto an Internet Relay Chat and used his personal IP address. Monsegur pleaded guilty to 12 computer related charges on August 15, 2011, and was threatened with a sentence of 124 years in prison. But he has since become an FBI informant and will likely be rewarded for this. The arrest of Sabu was immense for the FBI; however, several Anonymous "members" and sympathizers have reassured the public via twitter that "an idea cannot be killed."[12] And this is an important point. How can criminal justice agencies effectively take down a collective that remains hidden through anonymity and masks? They cannot. And they should. More importantly, Anonymous service a purpose that creates *good* for society through so-called *bad*. As dependence on IT and the Internet grow, governments will have to make proportional investments in Internet security, incident response, technical training, and international collaboration.[13] Nonetheless, the process will be indisputably complex and incredibly challenging for policing agencies to stay ahead of a younger generation born into an era of rapidly changing computing technologies. Moreover, there will be serious questions and social implications about whether or not government "protection" and law enforcement will preserve civil liberties and freedom online. We doubt this balance will be struck, but we hope that we will be mistaken.

A notable hack with tremendous impact occurred during the

holiday season in an operation entitled "LulzXmas." Hackers released 75,000 names, addresses, CCs and md5 hashed passwords to any customer that has ever paid Strategic Forecasting, Inc. In addition, they released 860,000 usernames, email addresses, and md5 hashed passwords for everyone who had ever registered on their website. Strategic Forecasting, Inc., more commonly known as Stratfor, is a non-governmental private global intelligence agency founded in 1996 in Austin, Texas. The privately owned company operates on a subscription-basis, for individual and corporate subscribes, by providing access to geopolitical analysis on international affairs. The corporation prides itself on gathering information via open-source monitoring and its global network of sources. Its founder, George Friedman, argues that Stratfor's work differs from other news sources, as theirs requires documented sources, research, logic and inferences. The intelligence organization media focuses on and records what is happening, why it is happening, and what will happen next (2012, n.p.)[14]. This hack was significant and posed a serious threat to the agency and to law enforcement. Members who hacked into the website also declared that on New Years Eve, they would hack into police department websites in order to protest the arrest of Chelsea (then Bradley) Manning. Manning was arrested in 2010 on suspicion for having released a controversial video, July 12, 2007 Baghdad airstrike, displaying U.S. soldiers killing 18 innocent civilians and journalists in Afghanistan to whistleblower website Wikileaks; moreover, she was suspected to have released 250,000 U.S. diplomatic cables and video footage of the May 2009 Granai airstrike[15] in Afghanistan. Manning faced a life sentence, and although her crimes were punishable by death; the prosecutors did not seek the death penalty. The case and trial was a serious issue for the soldier who leaked the cables. It is odd that in the Age of Information we punish the soldier who released the cables, yet we do not punish the soldiers in the videos who killed nearly two-dozen innocent civilians. The entire case has displayed throughout a military "don't ask, don't tell" policy. It is a serious miscarriage of justice to sentence a 22-year old soldier for leaking the cables when the documents do not appear to cause any imminent harm to U.S. soldiers. Furthermore, the events are several years old. There is a serious problem in sentencing a person to life if the U.S. army truly feels that what they are doing overseas is right and that the act, or mistaken enemy killing, was nothing to be ashamed of and simply an act of "collateral damage."

The question then becomes: how much information should be readily available to the public? Unquestionably, information that may contain "sensitive" information such as personal addresses or security information should remain out of the public light. Although, we believe that in the case of war, the more information that is accessible, the better. The public, especially in the United States, subsidizes an extremely large portion of the war. So much so that it has nearly bankrupted their country and destroyed their credit rating. If the public had access to raw unfiltered data and cables, perhaps the war would have been over years ago or perhaps the war would never have been supported in the numbers that it were. In any given war, governments lie. It is the only way to get the public on *their side*. Instead, the general population is bombarded by media companies serving corporate and hegemonic ideas that instill and identify the "enemy" as anything that falls under their definition of un-"American"; or any person who interferes with capital for that matter. And that is exactly what Chelsea Manning did. She created a gap between those capitalizing off of the profits of war and those who are paying the bills. In any situation, it is a lose-lose. The capitalists lose a hefty income source from the war and the public loses confidence in their governments as they churn out truthiness.[16] But maybe it's a good thing. Perhaps the masses of information available to us are paving the way for the Age of the Awakened.

Still, the public will only remain awake if the information is accessible, especially online. But as previously discussed, this is changing and it is changing at an alarming rate. Even though the some in Anonymous strive for anarchy, in fact what they have created is one of the most democratic systems in the world. In a sense, they have allowed anyone around the world to organize under an "Anonymous" banner and allow for people to express unfiltered opinions. The work that Anonymous engages in at times involves a criminal element; however, perhaps it is necessary for the idea to continue and in order for a new generation to steer away from the icebergs that lay ahead if governments continue to censor our free speech and spy on us online.

Without a doubt, the ideas laying behind the mask of Anonymous is something that governments, law enforcement agencies, and policy makers will have to pay attention to as the world moves further into the Age of Information. To date, countries around the globe have responded on a policy level to the threat of Anonymous by creating new laws around Internet usage, and several arrests have been made. But why is all of this important? The anonymous hacktivist group has interfered with and will continue to interfere with the production of capital. Even more problematic for some, Anonymous is an idea. As a result of their hacktivism, the costs of their political ends have cost industries millions of dollars; and there are no signs of them slowing down. Governments around the globe exist and survive by allowing for the ongoing production of capital by industries. When surplus value is under assault, companies and capitalists alike come forth and lobby the governments or law enforcement agencies to take action. This reality is not new. But the responses of these agencies will have to be reinvented. While logistically, it is one thing to go into a physical territory and arrest hundreds of people in support of an anti-globalization movement. It is more challenging geographically to target Internet hacktivists who hide behind masks and who possess a widening range of computing technologies. With politicians wrapping themselves in a flag, it equalizes Anonymous "members" hidden behind masks.

The big question then becomes: what lies ahead? The world is at a crossroads in relation to freedoms of speech and expression online. Up until this point, the Internet has served as an open exchange of knowledge and as a canal of intellectual development. But it is currently under threat. The dichotomy of ideas represents a foundational concept of expression and state control. On one hand, the crossroad can lead us further into the Age of Information and as knowledge expands at an exponential rate, people will enter into the Age of Awareness and governments may become more accountable or transparent. This new age will offer enlightenment and essential change, as societies become more informed — and more connected — while asking questions and challenging the current status quo. On the other hand, governments may travel down a path of suppressing their citizens. Personal freedoms and expressions will be placed under greater scrutiny, and a greater division will be formed between those who are working to maintain the status quo and those who strive for transference and knowledge. In any society, governments historically exist to control the masses. When groups of people become uncontrollable, or when persons challenge the established — through not agreed to — norms of society, state intervention can take place. The government and the bourgeoisie have always been afraid of labor and social organizations — albeit union organizations or social movements — and this will never change. When people organize and become too powerful; states expel their powers onto the opposing force and attempt to hinder them from drawing outside of the conventional lines of society.

If a person, or group of persons, establishes theory and actions that places capitalism under threat, these groups will consequently be silenced and deemed as the "enemy." But why does the government want to silence Anonymous? One answer may be that they threaten capitalism. Even more threatening, a generation has now grown up with the Internet and people today have infinite access to information. Unlike previous eras, people can readily gain access to a network that provides answers to pertinent questions, anytime. In relation to economics and private enterprise, a new generation seeks answers to their queries and challenges the philosophy of our so-called "free market." Communities are not buying into the same hegemonic ideals. But the challenge that lies ahead is establishing and uprooting a new social order that moves away from social inequality and the oppressing role of the state. Some fear that we are moving further into an era where "Big Brother" will be watching our every move. And this belief holds especially true today in light of the plethora of international Internet laws being passed or debated by governments. But there is a flipside to all of this. More and more people around the globe now have greater access to technology—most of which is Internet enabled—and the vast majority of the population is connected through a cyberspace medium. Although it is a metaphysical realm, information is being shared around the globe with a propensity for partnership. It may be true; the Big Brother may have their lenses set on infiltrating greater access into our personal and social lives. But the general public is looking back through the same infiltrating lens, except in the general publics situation, they are greater in numbers and do not adhere to the same legalistic or bureaucratic principles.

The tensions and disorders that culminate in any skirmish between the government and the laymen ultimately pave the way for change, good or bad. And that is what we are experiencing today as hacktivists are being forced to walk the plank as they fight against piracy laws, and Internet freedom of speech and expression. In many respects the communist manifesto is accurate in saying, "the weapons with which the bourgeoisie felled feudalism to the ground are now turned against the bourgeoisie itself."[17] And in a world dominated by technologies, it is likely that the enemy of the state will be hidden behind a mask or an Internet users smiling face. Perhaps if governments can steer a steady course between living in a society that promotes freedom of speech, future generations will be better able to move into an Age of the Awakened whereby knowledge is free and accessible. But until then, Anonymous will continue to engage in hacktivism and governments will continue to criminalize their actions.

Chapter 4

Applying For Netizenship: Foucault, Cybercrime and the Digital Age

There is a trust and distrust shared by citizens and governments. In the twenty-first century, contingents of both parties understand the power of an individual online. At present, international debate on cybercrime and the regulation of the Internet has commenced. Citizens of the Internet want online freedom, yet sovereign states have never advocated for a community without control of rules or conventions. This paper shall investigate how Michel Foucault's discussions on disciplinary power and governmentality can be applied to the online virtual community. Trends in both prevalence and incidence of cybercrime, as well as discussions on possible Internet regulations, will be explored. To date, the Internet has become a domain that has mobilized and radicalized the existence of online and offline communities. Much of the progressive online development is akin to those who challenge the constraints of modernity and a global commitment to security. Accordingly, efforts to qualm crime conducted via the Internet have been brought about through mechanisms of hierarchical observation, normalizing judgments, and examination online. The inherent confrontation and its consequence of online subjects have also created new techniques and strategies to respond to these circumstances by virtue of governmentality. As individuals continue to embrace the online virtual community, discussions of digital security and the role that nations assume will be of vital importance in the years ahead.

The Internet has come to be one of the most significant innovations of our time. The foundation of the information superhighway can be traced to precursors that date back to the 19th century, such as railways and telegraphs, along with other revolutionary technologies that led to booms and busts over the years (McLuhan 1962). Its formation can be attributed to military exploration, academic study and private investment. The driving force for new methods and measures of use online is largely accredited to computer programmers and hacker subcultures that explore uncharted territories, take risks, and break new ground. Prior to the age of information, power and knowledge were neither readily accessible nor arrangeable without significant time or expense. With an increase in diverse modes of wireless communication, people are connecting with distant environments on a level unparalleled in history. Without a doubt, the Internet has become a powerful tool for revolutionizing the way we think and how we live. In this day and age, society is impacted by the circular and reciprocal relationships between the online and offline environment. Accordingly, as globalization proceeds, digital and physical communities happen to mesh. The new circumstances for our contemporary way of life are redefining political and socio-cultural lines around the globe. The architecture of the information superhighway, however, like any community, is subject to risk, threat and vulnerability. At the present time, notions of community are changing as "individuality and privacy erode quickly in the search for power and profit" online (Mehta and Darier 1998, 108).

At present, one third of the world's population is using the Internet (ITU World Telecommunication 2011, n.p.). ITU Telecom estimates that 45% of the worlds Internet users are below the age of twenty-five (*ibid*). Moffitt's (1993) developmental theory, for example, might suggest that adolescents may therefore commit a larger portion of delinquent or cybercriminal activity. According to some, 52.4% of cybercriminals are between the ages of 18–30 (National Crime Records Bureau 2009). Aside from age, the study neither accounted for gender, ethnicity nor socioeconomic status. It also did not compare cybercrime in developing countries as compared to developed countries. This is important as opportunity for crime may be correlated to computer virtuosity and ability to access the Internet. Aside from cybercrime, we have seen a growth in cyber bullying, which can result in public harassment, alongside this cohort (Wolak 2004). It is likely that Hirschi's (1969) social control theory would suggest that these community members fail to maintain a bond with society consisting of attachment, commitment, involvement, and belief. In spite of this, those between the ages of 18–30 are enmeshed within the virtual online community. Accordingly, a solution to combat cybercrime may be to target networks that encourage and facilitate crime in such abandoned spaces whereby little regulatory authority or traffic is observed. With an increase in both crime and technology, felonious conduct online has become an important topic for discussion. Notwithstanding that criminal opportunity exists, social phobias of online use may increase as Internet usage becomes a central element of society.

Similar to the physical world, a large portion of crime facilitated through technology remains undetected and unreported as a result of computer virtuosity. In contemporary criminology, this hidden phenomenon can be understood as the "dark figure" of crime (Biderman and Reiss 1967). In terms of offline crimes, Skogan argues that "the problem is well known: an activity which is by some criteria a crime may occur without being registered in the systems devised to count it, thus reducing the accuracy of inferences from the data" (1977, 42). In relation to specific computer crimes, such as a zero-day attack[1] or acts of phishing[2], the problem, however, is largely unknown and unseen for a prolonged period of time. The undetectable and deceptive nature of these cybercrimes can be sufficient to cause harm to public and private databases. Along with the widespread harms to data contained within online community, computer malware can now affect physical systems beyond the realms of cyberspace. By way of illustration, the "Stuxnet" virus successfully destroyed 1,000 centrifuges as a part of Iran's controversial nuclear program (Williams 2012). In essence, newly developed cyber-weapons have the ability to attack physical infrastructure and have been referred to as the "digital equivalent of fire and forget missiles" (Milevski 2011, 64). Accordingly, liberal democracies need to address diverse security challenges as they are found in any large urban complex.

In the eighteenth century, precursors to the Internet materialized as the globe attained its "apotheosis in industrial modernity" (Mehta and Darier 1998, 107). Around this same period, legal regimes moved away from the cruel and capricious nature of law and punishment where people were "schooled in the lessons of justice, terror and mercy" (Hay 1975, 63). New power dynamics emerged in its place as governments moved toward increasingly administrative processes, bureaucratic procedures and scientific knowledge. With continuous change in our environmental, social and economic systems, communities are subject to new risks. Ulrich Beck argues how the world is in a period of second modernity whereby the globe is characterized through three criteria: indifference to national boundaries, space-time compression, and an increasing network-like interconnectedness between nation states (2000, 80). This understanding can be applied to the online virtual community. Accordingly, international citizens of the Internet are now able to connect across continents in real-time for a variety of purposes. This may correspond to both legal and illegal prospects. In the present climate, the skills and techniques of cybercriminals have made law enforcement an increasingly arduous task, domestic and abroad. The ability to commit crimes in one country against another sovereign state has also caused jurisdictional issues as cybercrime transcends borders. Moreover, cybercrime can be carried out with little effort. Appropriately, cybercrime should not be observed as a different phenomenon than crime opportunities that occur in everyday life (Felson 2002). By way of illustration, carrying out an illegal denial-of-service attack can be achieved with little technological skill by merely conducting an online search and downloading one of the widely available open source software. What is more, there are a plethora of services ranging from a virtual private network (VPN) to various circuits of encrypted connections, such as Tor, that make online identity anonymous. These technologies are the equivalent to wearing a balaclava for the purpose of concealing one's identity and gloves to avoid leaving fingerprints. These applications can be both helpful and harmful to society. By example, for those who reside within oppressive legal regimes, users are able to transmit information and data out of these restrictive environments with little risk for surveillance and monitoring. On the other hand, cyber-criminals may exploit these technologies that were created with pro-social and liberating aims. Nevertheless, as Felson argues, society can prevent crime by "supervis[ing] people, places, and things" (2006, 90). In spite of this, citizens of the Internet must be able to have confidence in those who monitor and conduct the supervision. The question becomes: how can society entrust those who survey and monitor online activity? In terms of services that render identity anonymous, "as a general rule, abandonment enhances crime by enabling anonymous intrusions" (ibid). Accordingly, the response should not be to criminalize users in cyberspace but rather to examine opportunities that give rise to deviancy. In sum, to render something illegal by reason of crime opportunity or misuse is unjust. The same tools that can have the potential for illicit use online also have the potential to "improve human rights across electronic media" (Oxblood Ruffin 2004). The amalgamation of our routine lives and the virtual online community, however, challenges previous conceptions of how man-made spaces can interact to provide social opportunity for crime (Newman 1972). And some Internet users, we suspect, have personal concerns and online social phobias as the information superhighway increases opportunities for crime as financial and confidential data become digitized and centralized to the web. That being the case, Foucauldian discourse analysis with focus on how controlling subjects within a territory, through mechanisms of disciplinary power and governmentality, can be applied to the online virtual community.

In the absence of theory, there is only opinion (Callender 2010). In order to understand how cybercrime and regulation of cyberspace may be debated, attention is paid to Michel Foucault's theory of disciplinary power and governmentality. Disciplinary power has its point of origin in the European Middle Ages whereby highly centralized sovereign power was exercised through law and military force. In modern society, it is manifested through a range of institutions and diverse disciplines that impact our daily lives. In essence, he argues that decision-making power has been directed away from a centralized sovereign power and toward diverse liberal democracies and their respective disciplines. Conversely, disciplinary power within the online community has been decentralized since the beginning. Although this may be subject to change as conversations surrounding the international regulation of the Internet have begun at the World Conference on International Telecommunications. This is unsurprising, as cybercrime knows no borders. Foucault (1977) argues that disciplinary power is exercised through three characteristics: hierarchical observation, normalizing judgments and examination. In regards to hierarchical observation, Foucault conceptualizes how Jeremy Bentham's permanent visibility prison, the Panopticon, served as a mechanism to produce "homogenous effects of power" (1977, 202). It was proposed that through environmental design, institutions could "make it possible for a single gaze to see everything constantly" (1977, 173). Consequently, subjects would self-regulate and manage their own behaviour to adhere to environmental norms. Bentham's idea served to legitimize and decentralize power through visible but unverifiable means for "the more constant, profound and permanent are its effects" (Foucault 1977, 203). In essence, disciplinary mechanisms in previous relations of sovereign power become the relations of discipline exercised by modern institutions. Discipline, however, only represents one way that power can be exercised. Foucault's progressive and modernist ideas were also implemented into military camps, working-class housing developments and educational institutions. His understanding can be applied to the online virtual world as "discipline works in an empty, artificial space that is completely constructed" (1978, 54).

For instance, within the context of an educational institution, use of online privileges subjects individuals to comply with institutional policies and regulations. In this environment, users of network and computer resources are responsible to comply with specific institutional bylaws. At this juncture, users of the Internet are susceptible to the gaze of information and educational technology departments. Meanwhile, students operate online in libraries and other public areas that subject them to the peripheral gaze of others. Academics have excelled for centuries under peer review and society should ensure that these advancements continue. This is challenging in an environment where hierarchical online surveillance and monitoring exists. Beyond education systems, a users Internet traffic can be monitored in real time by website data-mining software, Internet service providers and diverse regulatory authorities with or without a warrant. In essence, online disciplinary power operates through various control techniques, such as surveillance and monitoring, vis-à-vis virtual online systems. Notwithstanding that, the concept of disciplinary power arose out of the carceral system. It can be argued that operating online is a voluntary act, whereas a prison sentence improbably is not. Accordingly, rules and techniques of control are necessary or rather embedded within both the online and offline community, such as the carceral systems. Needless to say, it is becoming increasingly difficult to elude online use in business, personal communications, and entertainment. In spite of the potentiality for hierarchical observation, it is questionable whether or not users of the Internet regulate their own behaviour online as compared to those within a Panopticon. The questions then become: Should users of the Internet be subjugated to surveillance and monitoring? What are the subjective and objective expectations of privacy online? Are users of the Internet operating within a virtual Panopticon?

The second characteristic of disciplinary power is normalizing judgments. Foucault claims, "at the heart of all disciplinary systems functions a small penal mechanism" (1977, 177). By means of procedures and routines, it is theorized that techniques of control and training can produce expectations and standards for disciplinary subjects. Within the online community, the exploration of normalizing techniques for human judgments is readily visible within social networking services, such as Facebook. For instance, the amount of "likes" that a person receives may normalize judgments and create standards by which subjects are measured. As a consequence, a users public display of self may create a standard by which others also attempt to maintain. What is more, each individual user becomes a product of the Internet whereby others can analyze and describe. This may cause social phobias for some as one may feel as though they are being judged. It is, however, ironic as users of such social networking sites voluntarily subject themselves to the observation and judgment of others. These nominal forms of power may create standardized ways of operating online through the interaction between other users of the Internet, social networking sites, and third-party applications.

The final characteristic that disciplinary power exhibits is examination, which encompasses both micro-penalties and rewards. This particular form of disciplinary power combines the previous two techniques of hierarchical observation and normalizing judgments. It is attached to politico-juridical models that emphasize "disciplinary technology" (1977, 227) that bring micro-penalties and rewards into existence. This is achieved through "mechanisms of objectification", which in so doing, "we are entering the age of infinite examination" (1977, 187). Within the online community, the notion of infinite examination is ineludible as the expansion of new computing technology continues apace, and as our lives increasingly intersect with computer networking and the Internet. For instance, current increase in mobile phone use has created the circumstances to enable global positioning system (GPS) that can track location (Wiehe et al. 2008) and inertial navigation systems (INS), which enhances accuracy. Accordingly, cyber citizens and cybercriminals will respond to these new circumstances. These capabilities may also give rise to crime opportunities and exploits, although unintended and unforeseen. On the other hand, these forms of infinite examination pave the way for features that may prevent criminality or that may aid in locating people who require assistance from emergency responders, for example. Other forms of examination are visible online through Internet service providers that have the capacity to monitor and log real-time Internet traffic. As with anything web-based, there are helpful and harmful functions. For instance, such technologies may create a pathway for cybercriminals to travel to and fro, which puts users who fail to take precautionary measures at risk. Meanwhile, it also opens the door to conventions and arrangements that would allow regulatory bodies to implement forms of surveillance for unlawful online activity, such as Internet based sexual exploitation or financial and confidential data theft. To sum up, examination is inherent to the structure of the Internet given that everything is recorded and nothing is forgotten.

With the global spread of computing technology, governmentality has ascended into the realms of cyberspace. How society governs itself online is particularly important today as there are known and unknown risks associated with computer security. At present, law has been one tactic among many for reducing crime opportunity and targeting deviance. Another effect has been private industry, as software developers attempt to repel the latest cyber attacks and computer viruses. Within cyberspace, governmentality can apply to contemporary nation states targeting populations through "an explosion of numerous and diverse techniques for achieving the subjugations of bodies and the control of populations" (Foucault 1976, 140). Techniques of control online come from a variety of institutions and disciplines. For instance, online search engines are programmed to rank websites on the basis of popularity online and direct Internet traffic toward specific pathways while moving away from others. What is more, corporations may pay search engines in order to secure a more prominent position online. This mechanism is referred to as search engine optimization. Consequently, techniques of control position online nodal points that guide individual conduct that may influence "how power, knowledge, and subjects intermingle to create social forms, law, given truths, and so on" (Pavlich 2011, 139).

In 2012, a straightforward example of governmentality is illustrated by the Canadian government's attempt to garner public support through Bill C-30, the Protecting Children from Internet Predators Act. Under the guise of governmentality, the act is virtuous: protect children online. The title in and of itself should certainly be something that the public would support. When examined more thoroughly, the act contains clauses that would allow authorities to monitor real-time Internet activity and mandate Internet service providers to keep logs of their customers' online data. Additionally, the act does not require law enforcement or government authorities to possess a warrant. Some citizens may have confidence in the government, and Bill C-30, arguing that these are reasonable demands and circumstance in this day and age. Meanwhile, others may believe that they have nothing to hide from regulatory authority. Citizens may have every reason to trust their own government. Despite this, in the event that nation states cooperate to regulate cyber-space, the issue will be whether citizens of the Internet trust other countries with the personal data that their government may share. When attempting to push this bill forward, Canadian Public Safety Minister Vic Toews argued "either stand with us or with the child pornographers" (House of Commons, March 27 2012, n.p.). This example highlights the power of language within a given context to convey a particular message and to push for expansions of government online. This is also an exemplar of attempting to control a territory and the legal subjects within it via bringing online social phobias into play. This is a consequence of the ominous crime bill and the mechanics of governmentality. The modus operandi is compa-rable to the sovereign powers in the European Middle Ages that garnered power through legal sanctions and authoritative force; ruling the people and their property. In short, the attempt of controlling through governmentality online is to produce biopo-litical entities that promote ethical conduct and to set limits to regulate Internet access. Nonetheless, Foucault notes, "where there is power, there is resistance" (1976, 95). Foucault demon-strates how power can be obtained by the powerless through the very system that perpetuates their domination. For instance, he presents a chapel—Saint-Bernard—whereby Maoists staged a hunger strike and accomplished the aim of establishing a commission to study the living conditions of prisons in France (Miller 2000, 187). Equally spirited resistance can be observed online.

The most operative form of resistance within the online virtual community is computer virtuosity. As previously mentioned, there are a number of available tools at someone's disposal that allows him or her to operate online anonymously. This comes in the form of virtual private network, cryptographic systems, various operating systems and more. In the most basic sense, the above highlights techniques to evade governmentality and disciplinary power. The ability to operate online anonymously or without trace is similar to Plato's (360 B.C.E) text, "The Ring of Gyges", where the shepherd Gyges of Lydia discovers a golden ring that possesses the ability to render him invisible to others. Notwithstanding, these means are also the same tools available to disciplinary subjects who live in oppressive nation states that are attempting to unfasten current constraints of law and society. For this reason, worldwide efforts to rid of such services or render their use illegal will pose more harm than good. In any case, liberal democracies need to engage in rigorous debate in order to be able to carefully balance security and freedom online. Otherwise, the Internet may fall under the control of a users independent sovereign, which would thereby inhibit the ability to connect with others around the world.

Continuing ahead in the twenty-first century, society will increasingly intersect with technology. As crime and technology become progressively innovative, sovereign states and regulatory agencies need to develop diverse methods and techniques to target deviance. Accordingly, solutions for advancing security within cyberspace must be implemented through mechanisms that do not impinge upon reasonable expectations of online privacy. To date, the virtual online community has functioned without a central regulatory authority. This demonstrates how the ethos of the Internet, which is anarchic and open in nature, can also be cooperative and functional. Thus far, various disciplinary power techniques for social control have been implemented online. Meanwhile, notions of governmentality increase alongside as environmental, social and economic systems globalize the virtual online community. As important as it is for cybercitizens to operate freely online, it is equally important to be mindful of how cybercrime and its potential legal responses impact the openness of the Internet.

Chapter 5

Walking the Plank: Inciting Change through Whistleblowing

Everything is code and language. The power of code, language and of words is the ability to define, unite, and separate us from others and from ourselves. The word "whistleblowing" has conjured up an abundance of emotions and feelings over the years. Recently, this word has once again become a household noun, adjective and recurrent theme. Janet Near and Marcia Miceli (1985, 4) provide a straightforward definition for whistleblowing and define it as "the disclosure by organization members (former or current) of illegal, immoral or illegitimate practices under the control of their employers, to persons or organizations that may be able to effect action." Within the Canadian context, Kenneth Kernaghan and John Langford provide a broader definition of what constitutes whistleblowing within the public sector as "both the open disclosure or surreptitious leaking to persons outside the organization of confidential information concerning a harmful act that a colleague or superior has committed, is contemplating, or is allowing to occur" (1990, 94). The social determinants of whistleblowing and challenge of fostering the disclosure of dishonest or illegal behavior are particularly difficult to achieve. The treatment of the whistleblowers has also varied greatly throughout time and space. Going forward into the age of information, there is an imperative need to understand what has been discerned hitherto understood as whistleblowing, how whistleblowers can break new ground and how whistleblowers are (mis)treated.

Legislative Nodes: Sometimes Conducive, Sometimes Disparaging

The notion of whistleblowing is not unique to this generation. Needless to say, there are specific legislative nodes that highlight how whistleblowing has come to be conceptualized in the global North. In the early 1970s, Ralph Nader first coined the term as "an act of a man or woman who, believing that the public interest overrides the interest of the organization he serves, blows the whistle that the organization is in corrupt, illegal, fraudulent or harmful activity" (Nader 1972, n.p.). The definition provided by Nader is an admirable illustration of how whistleblowing can be carried out on an individual basis. The descriptive nature and scope of the term has undergone profound change, however, as societies have become interconnected at a level unparallel in history, largely due to ever-expanding technological capacity. Within the continental United States, the False Claims Act of 1863 carved a path for legislation enabling whistleblowing in order to combat the rising threat of corporate crime. During the American Civil War period, defense contractors were supplying the Union Army with deficient, fraudulent and hazardous products. Some well-known commercial examples dating from 1861 to 1865 include but are not limited to: gunpowder that had been salted down with sawdust, faulty rifles, and feeble horses in poor health (Lahman 2005, n.p.). The Act was ratified during this period to encourage ordinary citizens to come forward and reveal information pertaining to counterfeit goods and supplies purchased by the Union Army. The idea was simple: combat corporate fraud by gaining insider knowledge. In order to persuade and unveil wrongdoing, President Abraham Lincoln included a *"qui tam"* provision and reward system into the act (Beck 1999, n.p.). This permitted private citizens, unaffiliated with the American government, to come forth and file action against illegal or dishonest behavior on the governments' behalf. Within this provision, citizens were entitled to a reward between 15–25% of the recovery from a government lawsuit whereby the intelligence led to a conviction. Furthermore, whistleblowers were also at liberty to receive reparations for legal fees and other expenses that may have incurred throughout their process. At the inception of whistleblower legislation, state actors encouraged whistleblowing and paid workers who came forward to disclose acts of transgression. Critics of capitalism may view the False Claim Act as inherently exploitative and insulating for legitimizing state interests. However, the Act is meaningful as it recognizes that unscrupulous behavior should be made public. Since 1863, this line of thought has not profoundly change; however the treatment of whistleblowers has greatly varied when the matters in question are supportive of or opposite to government or private sectors.

A half-decade later: the Lloyd-La Follete Act (1912) was enacted to provide protection to civil service employees to criticized their respective agency and superiors. By allowing citizens to come forward and disclose information without fear of dismissal, the Act was put into practice under the First Amendment of the United States Constitution. Up until this point in time, the federal government was able to oust civil employees without due process (Smith and Gebale 1974). Consequently, employees feared that termination of employment was inevitable when evidence of wrongdoing is revealed. In essence, the Act secured their employment by preventing wrongful termination, which might otherwise be politically motivated. Similarly, in 2002, the Sarbane-Oxley Act was passed to protect whistleblowers at American corporations. This Act came about as a result of corporate and private accounting scandals pertaining to the cases of Enron, Tyco International, Adelphia, Peregrine Systems and WorldCom (Kohn et al. 2004). Section 1107 of the Sarbane-Oxley Act states that "whoever knowingly, with the intent to retaliate, takes any action harmful to any person, including interference with the lawful employment or livelihood of any person, for providing to a law enforcement officer any truthful information relating to the commission or possible commission of any federal offense, shall be fined under this title, imprisoned not more than 10 years, or both." Undoubtedly, the Act is useful for the governments to persecute wrongdoing within a private entity. Evidently, laws around whistleblowing have manifested around private and state interests. This is unsurprising, however, as hives of industries catalyze capitalist industrial growth. In respect to the brief aforementioned legislative overview, it is reasonable to assume that a government understands the impacts of whistleblowing. Yet, these laws fail to uphold to protection of whistleblowers equally. Concurrently, care of and legislation around whistleblowing greatly vary from nation state to nation state.

In respect to whistleblowing in Canada, the Law Reform Commission provides limited guidance to those in power at the upper and lower courts. In fact, there are only two considerations when a question of fact is presented via whistleblowing: (1) disclosure is justified only if the whistleblower has a reasonable ground for believing that a crime or civil wrong has occurred or will take place, and (2) that good faith on the part of the whistleblower must be proven (Ontario Law Reform Commission, 1985). One interpretation of the Commissions considerations is that that these standards are reasonable as it reduces the potential for individual or organizational harm that may, and can, arise from unreliable and invalid facts. Another interpretation may view this language as being demonstrative of the federal governments concerned for the protection of a wrongdoer, rather than the whistleblower him or her self. Undoubtedly, a reasonable grounds test is most useful in order to protect potential damage to reputation should there be a lack of sufficient evidence otherwise. However, it is this second consideration that becomes questionable in nature as it signifies a similar tone relating to whether or not a whistleblower is a reasonable person. In this sense, it is may be possible to dismiss that an employee was reasonable if the case of whistleblowing relates to surreptitious knowledge of harm as it often does. On that same note, it may state that public servants are not allowed to express their personal views on government policies (Kernaghan 2003). Consequently, it becomes extraordinarily challenging for a court to decide whether or not the disclosure is being imparted on the premise of concern for the public interest or whether it is motivated by personal statements. In the case that it is the latter, the whistleblower may face serious legal ramifications or termination of employment. In fact, in most cases, whistleblowers face significant reprisals or threats thereof (e.g., Daniel Ellsberg, Thomas Drake, Julian Assange, Chelsea Manning, or Edward Snowden).

Opaque Webs: Exposing Health and its Consequences

In Canada, whistleblowing legislation has fallen short of the United States and Europe. Paul Thomas (2005) notes that there are three principal forms of whistleblowing in the Canadian public and private sector: internal disclosure, authorized external disclosure, and unauthorized external disclosure. In his article, he examines how legislation surrounding the idea of whistleblowing has been designed to encourage and protect public servants to reveal dishonest and illegal behavior. This notion rings similar to America's False Claims Act (1863) and the Lloyd-La Follette Act (1913). On the other hand, Thomas warns that Canadian legislation is systematically designed to fail. Ultimately, he argues, the success of any law will be imparted by the political and administrative culture that supports the ethical awareness and responsible behavior in the daily practices of Canadian society (Thomas 2012).

In the late 1990s, Shiv Chopra's whistleblowing brought attention to one of the most significant incidents of federal wrongdoing in the public eye. Chopra, a microbiologist and human rights activist, and two co-workers, blew the proverbial whistle at the Canadian Senate's "Standing Committee on Agriculture and Forestry" in 1998 when they revealed how senior supervisors were pressuring their approval of multiple pharmaceuticals without rigorous testing. Among the pharmaceuticals in question was the drug "ciprofloxacin," which is largely used in cattle production today, as it was believed to be unsafe. Chopra warned to the federal government that the drug was unsafe and unsuitable as an antibiotic for both humans and animals. Despite the warning, the Canadian government approved the use of ciprofloxacin. Today, it is available and used in food production throughout United States, the United Kingdom, India, Spain, Pakistan, and Russia. Tragically, the drug has caused a death in the past few years (Adefurin 2011). In 2004, Chopra was fired from Health Canada. This case highlights how written legislation and courtroom practices can greatly differ. It is also demonstrative of elite deviance within Health Canada and the federal government as it pertains to corporate espionage, exploitation, and food processing. This is hegemony at its highest form as economic and political elites come to have society accept their negative and harmful behavior as regular and accepted routines of every day life (Gramsci 1971). This is also an example of surplus value at the expense of public health. Without a doubt, pharmaceutical industry assumes an important role in sustaining the Canadian and global economy. Consequently, there are certainly pressures to increase output in order to maximize profits. As a result, companies that are deemed necessary for the political economy are seemingly sanctioned to cut corners and operate with little fear of governmental regulation. In addition, some have argued how Canada's present conservative government puts the public at increased risk for health disease as deregulation of Health Canada inspection and food industries ensue (Lee & Campbell 2006, n.p.). In this instance, Chopra was carrying out the explicit directives upon which he was initially hired. Despite his best efforts, the government punished his actions by terminating his employment five-years later, although stating that it was due to a "lack of progress" on a project (Buckert 2004, n.p.).

In Europe, one of the most notable legislative acts is the Public Interest Disclosure Act of 1998. Prior the sanctioning of the Act, citizens in the United Kingdom (UK) were not protected from wrongful termination. The lack of the much-needed legislation for whistleblowers is highlighted in many instances. Stanley Adams, a corporate whistleblower, revealed in 1973 that price fixing was occurring with the product line for vitamins at the Hoffman-La Roche facility in Basel, Switzerland. Hoffman-La Roche is a Swiss-based global health care company in the pharmaceutical industry throughout Europe and abroad. When Adams came forward, the European Economic Community forwarded his name to his employer and he was charged with espionage, theft and unauthorized disclosure. Facing a prison sentence for several decades, his wife tragically committed suicide after hearing the news (Mathiason 2001). Stanley Adams, however, ended up only spending a few months in prison. Given the lack of legislation in the UK, the Public Interest Disclosure Act was enacted. Up until this point in time, it is plausible that members of the public were fearful from coming forward and revealing dishonest or illegal behavior in the workplace. Some might interpret the late enactment of this law's coming of age to be quite suggestive of capitalist society and state interests. Without a doubt, the Act is a useful piece of legislation for aiding workers within the community. Nevertheless, the UK is much older than its American and Canadian counterparts but yet it has failed to keep up with the rest of the working world in respect to legislation around whistleblowing. It might be argued that in the absence of such legislation, capitalism may have never formed to the extent to which it has. The Industrial Revolution was a period where technology, transportation and agriculture underwent profound changes in a short period in time. From the

Enclosures Act in the twelfth century to what some have called the 'second age of modernity' (Beck 2000), it can be argued that this lack of legislation may have created, to some extent, passivity among law makers and the public for enabling sustainable channels for whistleblowing and proactive disclosure of information. The past cannot be changed—for better or for worse—although the mediums available to whistleblowers have greatly improved with quickening pace of technological change and communication.

Transparency and Heresy: Inciting Change through Struggle

The Internet has become a marvel of our time. Not only has it revolutionized the way the think and how we live, but also it has restructured our ability to share and disseminate knowledge. Until recently, whistleblowing efforts had been largely confined by technological scarcity that required tireless effort. With new rises in technological capacity throughout the twenty-first century, whistleblowing mediums continue to evolve and become more communalized. One example is WikiLeaks: an international organization that operates as an online vehicle for members of the public to leak surreptitious knowledge and classified data. In late 2006, WikiLeaks made their website public and it has been a Mecca for intelligence enthusiasts, information activists and academics alike. The founder and director of the self-described not-for-profit medium is Julian Assange, a world-renowned hacker-activist from Australia. The WikiLeaks website offers a broad range of information that includes but is not limited to exposing: corrupt educational institutions, governmental secrecy and industrial fraud. Accordingly, governments and transnational conglomerates have paid close attention to their activities. This digital form of whistleblowing is unique in its approach as anyone with Internet access can make known private data with a simple click of a "mouse." And many do. In 2008, one of the most injurious leaks originated out of a collection containing nearly

400,000 cables dubbed the "Iraq War Logs." Among the cables were sets of documents pertaining to the death records of "insurgents," "enemy combatants" and civilians. The intelligence also exposed how American soldiers in relation to the occupation of Iraq had killed 66,081 civilians since March 2003. This is the largest data leak in the history of the United States military (Spiegel 2010, n.p.).

Whistleblower Inception and Legal Deception

A whistleblowers audacity is key to revealing unscrupulous questions or facts. The decision a whistleblower makes when leaking sensitive information should never be taken lightly. In recent years, it is understood that when a person decides to make private data public, the outcomes can lead to incarceration, termination of employment and perilousness. The story of Chelsea Elizabeth Manning (previously named Bradley Edward at time of arrest), a private first class intelligence analyst of the United States Army, is one such example where commitment to reveal wrongdoing within government resulted in just that. In 2010, Manning was arrested for publishing more than 250,000 U.S. diplomatic cables and 500,000 military reports originating out of the Iraq ("The Iraq War Logs") and Afghanistan ("The Afghanistan War Logs") war. One of the most examined leaks among the cables was a controversial video that depicted the wrongful killing of eight citizens and two war correspondents from Reuters by the United States military. In the eighteen-minute video entitled "Bagdad Airstrike/Collateral Murder," viewers witness military personnel execute innocent civilians in broad daylight using automatic weapons from an Apache helicopter. The justification for the killing was unadorned by American forces: their camera equipment was mistaken for automatic weapons (Cohen 2010, n.p.). In 2010, Manning was arrested and charged under a court martial while serving a tour in Iraq for suspicion of leaking classified materials to WikiLeaks.

Manning was incarcerated for more than 1,000 days before being on trial. Oddly, the Rule for Court Martial (707a) requires that the "accused be brought to trial within 120 days of referral of charges or imposition of restraint." Despite this, Manning was held under military orders, without trial, for over 1,000 days. On August 21, 2013, Manning was found guilty of espionage charges and sentenced to 35 years of confinement. Manning is currently being held at the United States Disciplinary Barracks at Fort Leavenworth, Kansas. The case of Chelsea Manning demonstrates forthright injustices within the federal policies and is detrimental to the historical purpose for which whistleblowing came about. The treatment of this type of political-whistleblowing highlights how legal frameworks can be overlooked and circumvented when "the facts" are in opposition to a legal regime. Importantly, the United Nations special reporter on torture has accused the US of cruel, inhuman and degrading treatment toward Manning (Méndez 2012, 76). Despite this, little has been done to improve her carceral condition. Moreover, those who kill innocent civilians overseas, and those who killed the reporters in the leaked film, face no harm or corollary for their actions. Perhaps the cases for the murderous soldiers were dismissed for being apart of "their job" or expected "collateral damage" that arises in war. In any case, a sense of injustice permeates the air.

From a critical perspective, the (mis)treatment of Chelsea Manning is not a surprising sequence of events. The wrongdoing revealed is in direct opposition to the government and to those who profit from war. This illustration is a straightforward example of how white-collar crime has pervaded various facets of capitalist culture as the government may empathize with those who fund wars. The exceptional dishonest and illegal behavior overseas has also been a justification for tightening up domestic laws in the United State; meanwhile, profiteers of war triumph from an untoward happanstance. However, a much more different picture is painted when a whistleblowers actions benefit the state. The case of Bradley Birkenfeld juxtaposes the features of Manning's condition at many levels. In 2007, Birkenfeld revealed that banks in Switzerland were aiding 4,700 American clients in evading taxes amid the United States. Without fail, the Internal Revenue Service (IRS) and the federal government were immediately paying attention to his insider knowledge. In the midst of further investigation, Birkenfeld was correct in his assumption. In September of 2012, Birkenfeld was awarded a generous $104 million dollar sum for his aid to the IRS and the American federal government (Kocieniewski 2012, n.p.). As luck would have it, he received this sum of money while serving a prison sentence for conspiracy to defraud the United States government. This instance highlights how a nations response will be contingent on whether or not the information is helpful or harmful to a legal regime. In Manning's case, the information reveals exceptional wrongdoing on behalf of the government and causes potential for profiteers of war to lose a considerable sum of money (should the war desist). In the meantime, persons responsible for wrongdoing remain unpunished while the whistleblower is incarcerated without trial. On the other hand, Birkenfeld—a convicted fraudster—was rewarded the largest sum to a single whistleblower in the United States history (Gonzalez, 2012, n.p.).

The contrasting treatment of Manning and Birkenfeld are two examples whereby reaction to dishonest and illegal behavior varied greatly and came about on an individual basis. Over the past decade, a much more communal force to expose harm has developed by using the technology, ideology and advocacy: the loosely affiliated hacker-activists, "Anonymous." Anonymous is a non-violent resistance movement consisting of a global collective of autonomous individuals who adhere to three basic principles: do not attack the media, do not attack critical infrastructure, and work for justice and freedom (Anonymous 2012, n.p.). Essentially, the group serves as a chaotic non-partisan that is united by two uncomplicated ethics: information should be free and accessible. Over the past few years, some have revered Anonymous (or Anons) in their online and offline activism. Anonymous, however, does not hold any central agenda. For this reason, they engage in various forms of illegal activity, legal activist activity and newly characterized forms of civil disobedience that include but are not limited to: whistleblowing, exposing online pedophiles, revealing corporate corruption, publishing state secrecy, and really, brining any miniscule or large-scale phenomena to light. In other words, some Anonymous persons believe they are making transnational despotic regimes—across all states and cultures—public. One method of Anonymous action is exemplified through computer hacking and community activism, or as coined by Omega and referred to by many, "hacktivism" (Oxblood Ruffin 2004, n.p.). Today, some believe that Anonymous echoes an insurrectionary anarchist tone as they openly advocate to ending state ascendancy and tyranny at any cost (Schwartz 2012b, n.p.). Acquisition to Anonymous is easy: be "Anonymous" by evading personal acknowledgment for hacking and activism. As a classifying phrase, Anonymous engages in global protests around the world, corporate and governmental hacks, and advocate for change in society on a day-to-day basis. Anonymous, unlike previous forms of whistleblowing, is unique for a number of reasons.

To start, the acts of whistleblowing are not accomplished on an individual basis. The acts are achieved through operative anonymity, either by wearing a Guy Fawkes mask in a real world protest, or by operating online through various mediums that ensure confidential data is not revealed. Secondly, the group discloses cases of illegal and dishonest behavior while simultaneously adopting an advocacy response. For example, by pointing the public in the direction of the wrongdoing and then proceeding to encourage protest through direct action achieves this feat of advocacy. This form of collective whistleblowing also juxtaposes Manning and Birkenfeld who chose to pass along the information but failed take an advocacy role. Although Manning may be an exception to this rule as it is nearly impossible to adopt this response while serving time behind bars. Nevertheless, Anonymous has remained a stoic supporter of Manning and has brought the case to the attention of the media by unceasingly discussing his mistreatment online (despite falling out with WikiLeaks). Thirdly, Anonymous does not often use any formal whistleblowing intermediary as a means to disclose cases of wrongdoing.

In the past and present, members of Anonymous have provided information to groups like Wikileaks. Although daily operations of the collective pertain to more immediate distribution networks: Twitter, Facebook, Pastebin, Anonpaste, and Internet Relay Chats (IRC). Without doubt, Anonymous has revealed numerous cases of wrongdoing over the years (see Olson and Coleman). Despite their immediacy and relevancy, their approach has its drawbacks. For example, Anonymous has served as its own judge and jury over the years. The strength to this approach is straightforward: it expedites the process of revealing cases of wrongdoing or illegal behavior. Whereas Anonymous decidedly takes action into their own hands, other groups and individual whistleblowers are constrained by law and society. A problem with publishing information by virtue of an online intermediary, as opposed to working within the confines of the criminal justice system, is the process of verifying the authenticity of the data. Proceeding by way of the criminal justice system, legal sanctions and an established burden of proof is required for a matter in question to proceed. In this regard, lawful gatekeepers exist to ensure that cases are substantial and legitimate thus reducing the potential for damage to reputation that likely ensues, should a case be brought to a courtroom. On the other hand, it is arguable whether or not cases whereby likelihood for conviction is low will ever reach a courtroom as such cases lead to public expenditures and reduced court efficiency. Similarly, a whistleblower may be paid by a wrongdoer to keep surreptitious information secret, as such; the public may possibly endure further harm.

Anonymous' approach to whistleblowing is excellent in terms of allowing information to surface, but there is a lack of checks and balances in place that aid in the validation and verification. On the other hand, the fact that the group works outside of the confines on the criminal justice system is useful as cases of whistleblowing may surface more easily and regulation to correct the dishonest behaviour may instead take place. Despite this, if the cases of whistleblowing are arduous to a legal regime, it is likely that the whistleblowers will not be meet with gratitude but rather legal persecution (see Tomblin and Jenion, forthcoming). This was the case for Chelsea Manning, and other members associated with Anonymous and Wikileaks.

Piracy and Privy: A Tentative Dispute

Within the past year, nonetheless, Anonymous and Wikileaks have begun to break apart over ideological differences. For decades, Julian Assange has asserted that information should be "free and accessible to all." This line of thought resonates among members of Anonymous and is one aspect of the community in which most are in agreement. In October of 2012, WikiLeaks went against their own statement of belief when they introduced a paywall that prevented the public from accessing any of the site's documents unless a donation was made. The decision has caused an incredible upset among some whistleblowers and Anons who feel that they "cannot support anymore what WikiLeaks has become" (Kravets 2012, n.p.). Consequently, Anonymous feels that WikiLeaks betrayed them, especially after coming to their aid in December of 2010 when MasterCard, Visa and PayPal barred the public from making donations. Adding further insult to injury, fourteen members of Anonymous have been indicted and are face fifteen years in prison for online protests defending Wikileaks and Jeremy Hammond. Hammond faces twenty years for allegedly supplying the Strategic Forecasting, Inc's confidential Global Intelligence Files relating to the U.S. presidential election. This example is demonstrative of how ideology can cause clashes between not only a wrongdoer and a whistleblower, but also among whistleblowers themselves as a result of opposing approaches. In order to combat WikiLeaks, Anonymous has started "Operation TYLER." Anonymous claims that TYLER is "a massively distributed and decentralized Wikipedia-style P2P cipherspace structure impregnable to censorship. TYLER will improve where WikiLeaks could not. In other words TYLER will be WikiLeaks on steroids" (Kovacs 2012, n.p.). In terms of WikiLeaks' decision to introduce a paywall forcing donations, it is apparent that the decision was made due to Julian Assange's ongoing court battles with the Swedish government. Assange is facing questioning in Sweden over alleged sexual assault allegations and has sought political asylum inside of the Ecuadorian Embassy in London since the summer of 2012. It is hypothesized that the sexual assault case has been conjured by the government in attempt to silence his whistleblowing efforts. Furthermore, Assange fears extradition to the United States is possible for WikiLeaks-related offences as he claims; "secret U.S. military documents indicate his life is at risk if he is handed over to the U.S" (Gill, 2012, n.p.).

From a critical perspective, it is indicative that the U.S. has been steering towards greater secrecy than any other period in history. Instead of a system build around openness and transparency, we have a system of opacity and seclusion. Whistleblowers are facing a war not only among themselves, but also among those whom they reveal dishonest and illegal behaviour against. One of the most alarming pieces of legislation against whistleblowers in contemporary society is the National

Defence Authorization Act (NDAA). It is hypothesized that NDAA will prevent some whistleblowers from coming forth and disclosing information and data that is vital to the public good as the U.S. government is now able to indefinitely detain citizens, journalists and whistleblowers. This decision is a move in the opposite direction of the False Claims Act, which rather than instilling fear among whistleblowers, it actually creates a reward system. Whistleblowers are vital to a nation when revealing surreptitious information and capricious workings of fate. If the government is unaware of corruption, it will never been fixed. Previous clauses for whistleblowers created protection and even encouraged private citizens to come forth. In contemporary society, governments appear to be moving in the opposite direction. Perhaps governments do not want to suppress corporate or internal corruption. Perhaps governments are well aware of the problems but are fearful of prosecuting individuals or corporations who ensure that the gross domestic product remains high. In any case, we are witnessing a shift in public opinion toward whistleblowers and the legitimacy around their work.

Leaking and hacking have gained notoriety, and public empathy, in recent times. While the characteristics of what "makes a good leak" are debated, it is understood that most whistle-blowers make private information known for the purpose of creating good, however defined. It is also argued that whistle-blowing does directly lead to personal benefit of the individual or improved quality of the life. Edward Snowden is one such example where someone who had authorized access to privy information decided to expose public malfeasances in hopes of diverting society away from its course toward panopticism (see the chapter on Foucault for more). In June 2013, Snowden leaked secret documents outlining US and European government surveillance programs to the press that were obtained while employed as a contactor for Booz Allen Hamilton, a technology-consulting firm. In particular, the disclosure details the National Security Agency's PRISM program that collects all "telephony metadata" between the United States and abroad by capturing "session identifying information... trunk identifier, telephone calling card numbers, and time and duration of call" (Foreign Intelligence Surveillance Court 2013, 2). Although the NSA outlines that the program "does not include the substantive content of any communication," (*ibid*) it should be noted however that "as few as four spatio-temporal points taken at random is enough to uniquely characterize 95% of the traces" in a fifteen-month study on human mobility data (Montjoye et al. 2013, n.p.). In response to the leak, the US government has pursued Snowden for making public the realities of the digital panopticon in which we live. As a consequence, Snowden took flight toward Europe as a result of a lack for proper American whistleblower protection and is currently seeking asylum at the time of this publication.

Conclusion

The severity in state responses to whistleblowers has been increasingly hazardous over the years. Generally, the ideas surrounding unauthorized disclosure of information pull people in opposite directions. The evolution of legal history in Canada and the United States highlight how specific legislative nodes have encouraged or restricted efforts to make private infor-mation public. As technology and state-corporate crime continue apace, it is certain that there will be a greater need for whistle-blower protection in order to elicit change and to construct trans-parency within society. With diverse communities at the forefront of shaping a new electronic frontier, it is hypothesized that communal whistleblowing efforts will increase in number and scope. After all, it is only through openness and trans-parency from the state that we will be able to move from an Age of Information to an Age of Discussion.

Chapter 6

Against the Online Enclosures:
For a Cyber Commonism

Some anarchists and libertarian Marxists have offered analyses arguing that the growing application of property rights to knowledge and creativity, and the use of state surveillance and punishment to secure that property, is in fact a new enclosure movement, similar to the enclosures of common land during the period of capitalism's early emergence from feudalism. Indeed it might be suggested further that an increasingly vigorous application of the language of property rights to knowledge and creativity, and extensions of state surveillance, represents an enclosure of the mind.

If the imposition of property regimes on knowledge and creativity constitutes what might be viewed as a second enclosure movement, then one might ask, what is emerging as the equivalent of the Diggers or Ranters who stood against the first enclosures? Against more pessimistic accounts of the new enclosures, social theorists John Clippinger and David Bollier (2005) suggest that the growing global movements for free software herald the beginnings of a renaissance of the commons. The anarchists of TAO Communications as well as Anonymous and LulzSec provide ongoing examples of what the new Diggers or Ranters might look like. At the same time current, and proposed, international trade policies as well as security programs such as NSA pose tangible threats to the future of the knowledge commons, cyber collaboration, and mutual aid.

An important aspect of the knowledge commons is that many participants in the various collectivities are workers in a variety of institutions. This was a key realization that motivated the practice of TAO organizers, as is explored in the final chapter.

While so-called computer "geeks" (well-educated youth from middle class backgrounds) do play a significant part in the networks, they are not even the majority of participants (Cleaver 1992).

Some theorists (see Dyer-Witheford 2010) use the term commonism to describe the current impulse against enclosure. The notion of commonism speaks to the desire for (and the reality of) collective ownership and collaborative labor without invoking the failed experiments of Soviet-style Communism (or Leninism).

On the Commons: Common Resources, Common Struggles

The notion of the commons refers to the collective lands and resources upon which humans have depended for survival (along with other species) over the course of generations (or life on this planet as we know it). The commons suffered a range of enclosures (by twin mechanisms of law and force) as capitalism has spread from the late-feudal period to the twenty-first century.

The struggle over the commons has been an ongoing feature of capitalist societies from the inception. It might be understood that in the contemporary context the commons expresses the possibility of collective ownership in three primary social domains (Dyer-Witheford 2010, 106). These are ecological commons (water, lands, forests, atmosphere); social commons (welfare, health, education, housing); and communications commons (publications, internet, social media, mobile technologies). Cyber disobedients fight largely in the domain of communications commons, but they are often engaged in actions to defend the other commons simultaneously (in defense of ecology, against corporate and military despoilers) or social commons (in defense of intellectual freedom and education or housing and health care).

The spheres of human life—the commons—intersect and reinforce. The social commons sustains the communication commons, allowing for the educational infrastructures, health, and shelter necessary for development of the web and equitable access to it. At the same time, the communication commons— human connectivity or solidarity—provides the basis for collective defense of the other commons. Dyer-Witheford offers an example of the circulation of flows through the commons: "Let's suppose that a publicly-funded education institution (social commons) produces software and networks that are available to an open source collective (networked commons), which creates free software used by an agricultural cooperative to track its use of water and electricity (ecological commons). This is a micro model of the circulation of the common" (2010, 110). The elements circulating within these commons are not commodities. They are produced primarily as specific use values. Neither are the exchanged for profit. The basis of distribution is more one of mutual aid or simply the free interchange of knowledge.

Capitalism is a system based on the production of commodities for exchange and profit. The commodity privileges exchange value (profitability) over use value (human need). Within a commonist society, the emphasis is restored to use values and human needs. The basis for this is the commons—the sharing of resources. This is a collective process—the commons enlarges connectivities and collectivities. It does not assume private ownership and enclosure of resources (by those who seek to gain profit in unequal exchange).

In the web, as in society, the forces of commodity and commons are thrown into ongoing conflict (a conflict that has always been at the dialectical heart of the capitalist mode of production). These conflicts have, despite, general under-standings, marked the web from the very beginning of personal computerized networks. Nick Dyer-Witheford describes the dual aspects of the struggle over the communications commons as follows: "Capital is attempting to repress these developments — through incessant anti-piracy sweeps and intellectual property (IP) battles — or co-opt them. But alternatives beyond what it will allow are expressed in 'creative commons', 'free cooperation' and 'open cultures' movements contesting the intellectual property regime of the world market" (2010, 108). This is the proper context for understanding cyber disobedience. Popular accounts tend to provide this struggle, what might be called a dialectical one, in a one-sided fashion.

Cyber anarchists seek the extension of the communication commons, through shared production and distribution. The web is viewed by cyber anarchists as a form of common wealth. It also provides important—one might even say necessary—means for preserving and restoring social and ecological commons— through knowledge sharing, research, collaboration and problem solving. The collective use of resources allows for the defense of the ecological commons and lessens the impact on the environment caused by the large scale production of technology for privatized or individualized use. At the same time:

> A network commons in turn circulates information about the condition of both ecological and social commons (monitoring global environmental conditions, tracking epidemics, enabling exchanges between health workers, labour activists or disaster relief teams). Networks also provide the channels for planning ecological and social commons — organising them, resolving problems, considering alternative proposals. (2010, 110).

Cyber anarchists affirm the commons in face of attempts by states and capital to enclose or privatize the shared labors of the web, to throw up fences and borders dissecting, or managing, connectivity and free circulation (of ideas, practices, resources). The commons is based on openness. For cyber anarchists, the defense of openness speaks beyond the communication commons. Openness is a more extensive political position against enclosure and borders. Thus, many cyber anarchists work on behalf of, as part of, broader struggles against borders and the flow of people from place to place. They target statist systems of control and closure, surveillance, regulation, and restriction in defense of the mobility of the working classes and the poor. If, in a supposedly global age, capital is free to circulate globally, why not labor, they ask.

DIY Production: Challenging Capital

Autonomist Marxist theorist Antonio Negri notes that the model for postmodern production is linguistic cooperation—it is communication (2008, 161). Negri points out that contemporary machines cooperate through language and via language original forms of cooperation are ever emerging between and among individuals. Linguistic cooperation is a necessarily productive cooperation, for Negri (2008, 161). Thus, we need always to ask, what is the articulation of command within these flows. For cyber disobedients this is the crucial question. How can the multitude (or the working class from another perspective) be a constitutive force within this? How can it articulate commons against property? There are differences between the activities and desires of the manager and the worker. For Negri, that which distinguishes is the common. He states:

> This is what enables us to divide the manager from the worker: in fact it is only the affirmation of the 'common' which permits us to understand the flows of production from within and to separate the (alienating) capitalist flows from the flows that are recompositional of knowledge and freedom. The problem will thus be resolved through a break at the level of practice, one which can reaffirm the centrality of common practice. (2008, 162)

The do-it-yourself (DIY) networks of the web have raised possibilities beyond those of distribution. They raise, fundamentally, issues of the reorganization of production along lines of control by workers themselves. For Dyer-Witheford: "Peer-to-peer networks and free and open source software movements have taken advantage of the possibilities for the reproduction of non-rivalrous goods and collaborative production to generate networked culture whose logic contradicts commercial axioms" (2010, 108). This brings the activities of the communication commons close to the heart of capitalism, and raises the possibility of a real struggle to end or surpass the capitalist mode of production. Here is a fundamental contradiction, as suggested by Marx, between the means of production and relations of production constrained within an obsolete productive structure that constrains social development.

For Nick Dyer-Witheford, the failure of the market in network domains appears as the inability of capital to adequately use the new technological resources (2010, 108). As Dyer-Witheford argues: "Networks show the market's inability to accommodate its own positive externalities, that is, to allow the full benefits of innovations when they overflow price mechanisms" (2010, 109). The innovations of the web—and growing capacities for immediate circulation of knowledge and communication have been developed outside of the market (2010, 108). As Dyer-Witheford suggests: "Capital's contribution has been to try and stuff these innovations back within the commodity form, realising their powers only within the boundaries of information property and market pricing. But digital innovation has persistently over-spilled these limits" (2010, 108). These contradictions, and the inefficiency of capital's efforts at enclosure, show the strains in capitalist social development and suggest the early stages of transformations to a new social arrangement. New connectivity and innovating relations of production, and rapidly developing means of production, strain against the limits and constraints of capitalist ownership and control.

Not only does this raise issues of ownership and control of production. More pressingly it actively poses the challenge, and possibility, of workers' control once again. For Summer and Halpin: "The logic of autonomy allows the components of the system to optimise their own connections, and so connect to people, materials, passions, and places in manners that takes [sic] optimal advantage of material and energy flows. Production is linked to a logic, not of growth, but of satisfying needs through 'commons'" (2010, 119). There is political potential of freedom of the multitude in these processes. It is only potential, however, an undecided outcome. For Negri:

> This is very much an open question, and it means that we have to elaborate new ideas, and in particular analyse the *mechanisms of cooperation which are formed within, and extended via, the networks*. Do forms of productive cooperation exist, in terms of freedom (and hence a cooperation which has no boss and does not have the necessity of transferring the ability to produce onto some capacity for command. (2010, 103)

Recently there has been a resurgence of efforts to pursue some of the *productive* potential of the web. As Dyer-Witheford suggests: "Increasingly, however, free and open source software and P2P constitute an electronic fabric of production, equipping people with a variety of digital tools for everything from radio broadcasts to micro-manufacturing" (2010, 108). One might reflect again on the struggles of Cody Wilson and his 3-D gun.

One ongoing outcome involves transformations at the level of the state. For Negri: "In matters of culture, language and media too, the nation-state no longer enjoys centrality, because it is continuously traversed by antagonistic currents and by a multiverse of linguistic and cultural inputs that deprive it of the possibility of asserting itself as hegemonic and as exercising command over the cultural process" (2008, 4–5). There is an interconnection between a revolution in production and a linguistic revolution (Negri 2008, 103). Negri notes that meaning is born from linguistic cooperation (2008, 103).

As suggested above, the common is constructed in processes of antagonism. Knowledge and action converge in figures of militancy (Negri 2008, 162). This implies, as discussed in the "Introduction," that movements must break from the confines of legality and taken for granted assumptions about political action (and proper forms and sites of action).

Cyber anarchists confront a new composition of labor (and the working class). This is based in the new connectivities of (re)production and circulation in the Net Age. This (re)composition is in flux as an expression of struggle. Enclosure and the commons. Commodity and communication.

Current crises, especially of global environments and the natural world, show the insufficiency and incompetence of the so-called "free market" as a means of social planning (Dyer-Witheford 2010, 107). The response required to address ecological crises (from instant reduction of greenhouse gas emissions, to transportation changes, to de-militarization and production changes) cannot be achieved through mechanisms that privilege profit over ecological (including human) needs.

Future Possibilities/Potenza?: Complexity, Networks, and Change

For certain cyber anarchists there is some engagement with complexity theories and a sense that capitalism, rather than a uniform technological system (a la the Unabomber) is actually governed by non-linearities. Different parts are linked in dynamic networks (and flows).

As Summer and Halpin note: "This means that sometimes a small event causes a small reaction in the system, but at other times a similar event can have a massive effect" (2010, 113). The non-linearity of capitalism is reflected in the various crises that wreck the system so frequently, if irregularly. Some are caused by relatively routine or minor actions (such as mortgage lending practices or investment decisions) which would otherwise have little impact—and may occur comparatively quite frequently. This all leaves cyber anarchists with a certain degree of optimism that the capitalist system is not as monolithic or as persistent, and resistant to anti-capitalist change, as it often appears.

Some cyber anarchists would suggest that the massive increase in energy and materials in the global internet age coincide with deepening ecological crises, and that these together (and extended rapidly over space and time) suggest conditions that could mean the end of capitalism as it is known. They are quick to point out however that nothing is assured. There will certainly be, as there have already been, attempts to preserve capitalism (private ownership and exploitation) through various schemes of "green capitalism."

Regenerating complex systems, like the internet, are open and require new inputs of energy and materials (Summer and Halpin 2010, 114). As Summer and Halpin suggest: "For the internet to be maintained, for example, broken computers must be replaced—materials and energy need to flow—otherwise it decomposes and stops being a complex system" (2010, 114). For cyber anarchists:

The internet is more than a collection of computers. This is because the configuration of the connections is important. Complex systems involve many connections between components that form loops of interaction. This contrasts with many hierarchical systems where the interactions between the various components are deliberately minimised. It is the feedback loops involving these connections that can change the system as a whole. So-called negative feedback loops tend to keep the system in its current state, while positive feedback loops may push a system to a new state, or new type of system. (Summer and Halpin 2010, 114–115).

The notion of commons changes rapidly as connections and flows increase, new intersections emerge, and networked connectivities expand over space and time. This is perhaps especially so in the context of technological infrastructure like the internet and the emergence of mobile technologies with which the net has merged (Summer and Halpin 2010, 118). These are imaginal and ideational as well as practical and physical connections.

As conditions change, the regular(ized) purposes to which the technologies are used and networks initiated change. As Summer and Halpin suggest:

> In periods of stability people use such technologies to do the things they normally do in stable situations: flirting, say, but via text messaging. But when our very survival is at stake, or when we catch a glimpse of a much better future, people can use these technologies for extraordinary goals, to mobilize globally in a sophisticated manner never before seen in history. (2010, 118)

Cyber anarchists seek to extend the participatory, decentralized, and collaborative configurations such that resources can flow in a way that is freely exchanged and engaged. Their view is one of a tech commons based on the free movement of knowledge and the self-determined labor of tech producers. This is an impetus against and beyond privatization and the state capitalist control of the web.

Control Matters

The anti-technology/anti-civilization approach fails to analyze capitalist forms of ownership, control, and scarcity. Conversely, for cyber anarchists, if resources taken from the useless production of exchange values were simply left alone or used solely for positive technological purposes and procedures then some aspects could be preserved and others transformed or abandoned entirely in a way that would be resource conservators or energy savers.

The section covering paragraphs 111 to 113 of the Unabomber Manifesto is titled "Industrial-Technological Society Cannot Be Reformed." Freedom, in his view, cannot be rescued without sacrificing the benefits of technology. The section covering paragraphs 121 to 123 clarifies further. That section is titled "The 'Bad' Parts of Technology Cannot Be Separated From The 'Good' Parts." For the Unabomber, but not for cyber anarchists, modern technology is a unified system in which all parts are dependent on and reflect one another integrally.

In the view of the Unabomber, the technology is a more powerful social force than the aspiration for freedom. But anarchists counter that the aspiration for freedom is really thwarted by capitalist forms of ownership and control of technology (and land, water, resources, necessities). Even the issue of what technology is produced is a matter of ownership and control—of decision-making authority—not technology per se.

Against Authoritarianism

The current period of crises, expressing the confluence of massive energy and material expenditures and natural ecological limits suggests a period of necessary transformation. It does not suggest what form the transformations will take—better or worse.

This could be a period of transitions to new system(s)—new society (Summer and Halpin 2010, 119). In such periods there is always the possibility for convergence around an authoritarian response. Some form of fascism may re-emerge as an attempt by elites to extend systems of surveillance, command, and control over resources and populations. Some aspects of this option can already be glimpsed.

Cyber anarchists (in some cases alone) are aware of an active against these authoritarian extensions. Indeed, they have been at the forefront of the struggles to assert or defend a commons against the expansion of authoritarian reach and attempts to enclose public resources and networks—human connectivity. In the face of corporate privatization and neoliberal government policy initiatives against the socialization of technology, cyber anarchists mobilize. Acts of cyber disobedience are at the front lines of struggles over emergent systemic formations. While techno-fascism seeks to reduce, break, and/or control connections, cyber anarchism is based on the extension, expansion, and strengthening of connectivity.

This marks cyber anarchism as distinct from previously dominant revolutionary formations of the political Left in contexts such as Britain and North America, particularly Leninism and its variants. These new movements are decentralized, horizontalist, and non-determinist. At the same time these are attributes that characterize many of the movements of the period of resistance to globalization, including indigenous movements and poor peoples' movements, North and South, and the occupied factories movements of the global South. Clearly the forms of the networks are resonating throughout social contexts.

Cyber anarchists see networks and decentralized technology as offering possibilities for pluralistic and autonomous decision making and social planning. Autonomous assemblies networked in a federative relationship can plan as well as providing an active and participatory practice to guard against and fend off bureaucratic manifestations Diversity is represented in the autonomous assemblies while multiple DIY connections encourage innovation. As Dyer-Witheford notes:

Commonism scales. That is, it can and must be fought for at micro and macro, molecular and molar levels; in initiatives of individual practice, community projects and very large scale movements. If the concept is at all meaningful, it is only because millions of people are already in myriad ways working to defend and create commons of different sorts, from community gardens to peer-to-peer networks. (2010, 112)

The communications commons opens opportunities for a new system based on connections of affinity—much like the early web, and like the historic movements of anarchy itself. For this approach production is cooperative and self-determined rather than based on private command. For Summer and Halpin: "Production and decisions about production are made via direct democracy—which maximises connectivity. Moreover, this highly flexible system of autonomy, collectivity and commons may well allow us to confront the ecological crisis" (2010, 119–120). These relations have a high degree of intensity, activity, and feedback.

For cyber anarchists the free flow of knowledge and cooperative production will be asserted in responding to current and coming ecological and social and economic crises, as many are today. Yet new opening will emerge and be developed for additional and improved initiatives. Those systems that allow for quick and mobile solutions to problems will have some real, pressing, necessity.

Rethinking Democracy

Anarchists in general recognize, with philosopher Slavoj Žižek, that "representation always acts as a violent *intervention* into what it represents" (1998, n.p.). Democracy has consistently, and conservatively, been conflated with representative parliamentarism. As Corcoran (2011) notes, representation is not a form of government necessary to technologically and socially complex societies.

As Corcoran suggests, the capitalist context "is structurally incapable of recognizing the capacity for proletarian innovation which inhabits everyone" (2011, xii). Innovation is always presented as the purview, and more importantly the property, of capital. Corcoran notes that there is no necessary link between states of society and forms of politics as is often claimed by the oligarchy that enjoys, and benefits from, the current arrangement of things (2011, xxi). For Corcoran: "'Representative democracy' is the political form that has come to prevail more or less unimpeded thanks to the weakening of egalitarian inventiveness and a general submission to the blind power of the economy" (2011, xxi). This is in many regards an effect of power that has excluded and marginalized or denigrated alternatives.

Following Alain Badiou, we might suggest that the struggles of cyber disobedients over the communications commons, in the end, reveal the incommensurablity between power and thought. The distance between the state and truths. Of the distance between power and truths (between state and creative thought) Alain Badiou states: "In the end, power is violence, whereas creative thought knows no constraint other than its own immanent rules" (2011, 6). Democracy, despite its own claims, is violence.

Immediatism: Theorizing Resistance to Enclosure and the "One World" of Capitalism

The publication, in 1985, of *T.A.Z.: The Temporary Autonomous Zone, Ontological Anarchy, Poetic Terrorism* signaled the arrival of Peter Lamborn Wilson's mystic alter ego Hakim Bey as an influential voice in the recent renewal of anarchist theory. In the years since the publication of *T.A.Z.*, Bey's work has proved both immensely influential and controversial. Indeed, the debates it inspired in the pages of major anarchist magazines, including *Anarchy* and the *Fifth Estate*, as well as in various zines (do-it-yourself publications) within the anarchist *milieu* were among the most lively in anarchist circles in decades. Younger anarchists, and those new to anarchism, took Bey's call for "poetic terrorism" as inspiration for the waves of "@-zones" (anarchist infoshops, community centers, art and music spaces) which emerged especially in urban neighborhoods across North America in the 1990s. Others (most notably Murray Bookchin) condemned Bey for supposedly offering up apolitical "postmodern" bohemianism in the guise of anarchism. Wherever one stands *vis à vis* Bey's vision of anarchy, however, there is no question that his work continues to pose a creative and intelligent challenge to traditional notions of what constitutes critical theory and radical politics in the new millennium. In particular his thinking on the web, and networks within the web, and his notion of pirate utopias, has influenced cyber activists of various stripes. Indeed collections have been devoted to discussion of some of Bey's notions in the context of web practices (see Ludlow 2001).

For Bey, the future of radical political ideas and practices (and the future, or non-future, of what used to be called the political Left) remains at the forefront of concerns for contemporary anarchism in the context of neoliberal globality. In a number of publications that have been widely read and influential within anarchist circles Bey discusses the prospects for resistance to what he terms "too-late capitalism," the mono-culture of global capitalism. Among his consistent preoccupations is "the revolutionary potential of everyday life" (1996, 7). Rather than focus on a revolutionary or post-revolutionary future "after the revolution" his call is the act as if the revolution is already underway—to be revolutionary immediately. His primary concern rests with the possibilities for multiplying the secret or clandestine spaces in which enclosure and commodification might be avoided and the creative powers of everyday life (re)affirmed.

Much of Bey's writings, especially his book *Millenium*, revolve around his view that capitalism, with the collapse and discrediting of socialism, has finally conquered the world. From his vantage point: "Capitalism is now at liberty to declare war & deal directly as enemies with all former 'alternatives' (including 'democracy')" (1996, 52). For Bey, there is no longer a "third path," (or third way or Third World) since the second (Communism) has disappeared. According to Bey, the newly enthroned "one-world" (of money and finance capital) obliterates space and presence reducing complexity to sameness. Almost everything enters into representation in the late capitalist "empire of the image" (of which money is the exemplar). For Bey, this leaves us with a simple choice: "either we accept ourselves as the 'last humans', or else we accept ourselves as the opposition. (Either automonotony or autonomy)" (1996, 30). Neutrality is no option and for Bey the only way out is anarchy.

While, on the surface, seeming to echo neoliberal "end of history theorists" such as Francis Fukuyama and Daniel Bell, Bey is not yet ready to yield to their hubris. The one world's claims are, after all, spurious. There is always possibility for escape, opposition, rupture. Every enclosure has an outside, "not to mention a liminality around every border, an area of ambiguity" (1996, 35). It is here that the uprising, the opposition, finds *its* "heartland."

In a short essay in *Millennium*, "For and Against Interpretation," Bey decries capital's monopoly of interpretation in the one world. This monopoly results in a "scarcity of interpretation" (1996, 60) for the rest of us which renders us as objects within the interpretations of (capital's) authority. Not only does it mediate our material transactions, capital stands between us and awareness. Everything must be mediated by money; nothing ("not even air, water, or dirt") is to be experienced outside of this mediation ("the exacerbated mediation of a power that can only grow by creating scarcity and separation," 1996, 64). Against capital's monopoly, Bey renews classical anarchist calls for self-creativity, and convivial meaning production. No interpreters (revolutionary or otherwise), only companions in networks of reciprocity. This is, once again, a call for self-production of a commons.

For Bey, and this is a point taken up by subsequent anarchist writers such as Heidi Rimke and Richard Day, only lived experience (affinity, self-produced desire) can present another world beyond the enclosures of money. In Bey's view: "The 'spirituality of pleasure' lies precisely in a presence that cannot be represented without disappearing" (1996, 32). Bey rejects the claims of advertisers that capital can satisfy desire. Instead he follows Walter Benjamin in arguing that capital, rather than liberating desire, only exacerbates longing. According to Bey: "Capital liberates itself by enslaving desire" (1996, 32).) Against the hermetism of the one-world "risk society," its management of desire and imagination, its dread of carnality, Bey advocates "a reenchantment of the forbidden" and a return to the senses (taste, touch, and smell against odorless mass industrial civilization). Eros must escape the enclosures, or we must rescue it!

Fortunately, resistance to "the Market" of capital persists in gift economies of reciprocity, mutuality, and redistribution (in do-it-yourself, DIY, cultures and underground economies). Drawing upon the economic work of Karl Polanyi and the anthropology of Pierre Clastres, Bey highlights the resistance that has met every threat of "the Market's" emergence. In keeping with an anarchist perspective Bey looks to the "self-made aspect of the social," DIY, a spontaneous ordering of reciprocity, as expressing a "non-predatory expansiveness," a "convivial connectivity," an "eros of the social" (1996, 42–43). The one world is never alone; the archaic presence of revolution still stands as its Other.

The hegemonism of the one world leads Bey to retreat from his earlier postmodern enthusiasm for aesthetic withdrawal ("disappearance as will to power") as a mode of resistance, however. In the new millennium there is only capitulation or opposition and Bey is now clear that flight, far from offering an instance of resistance, is now marked primarily as an instance of capitulation. This does not diminish the tactical importance of clandestinity, however; the secret remains revolutionary in its escape from absorption into the totality.

Of great, if often overlooked, significance for a rethinking of contemporary commonist approaches are the under-appreciated and largely misunderstood writings of Max Stirner and Gustav Landauer. One detects a uniquely Stirnerite presence in Bey's work in particular. Like Stirner's self-confident, unconventional "egoist" the anarchist of the TAZ awaits no salvation by abstractions such as "the future" or "the revolution." It waits for no Idea (whether anarchism, socialism, or some other) to free it. The immediatist strategy of creating alternative futures in the present or autonomous zones is reminiscent of Stirner's appeal to insurrection rather than Revolution. As Peter Marshall suggests:

> The Revolution aimed at new *arrangements*; insurrection leads us no longer to *let* ourselves be arranged, but to arrange ourselves, and sets no glittering hopes on 'institutions.' It is not a fight against the established, since, if it prospers, the established collapses of itself; it is only the working forth of men [sic] out of the established. (Marshall 1993, 638)

As for many anarchists at the turn of the millennium, Bey locates the most (indeed at the time the only) interesting beginning of this rethinking, once more, in the EZLN, the Zapatistas, in Chiapas. The EZLN is interesting both because it found its inspiration beyond the "Internationale" (because it appeared at the same moment the USSR disappeared), and because it was the first revolutionary movement to define itself against "global neo-liberalism." Chiapas was, according to Bey, the first revolution of the new millennium. Others have, of course, followed, from the post-Seattle alternative globalization uprisings, to the factory recuperations of Latin America, to the Arab Spring, to Idle No More. Yet each of these has drawn from and expanded upon practices and perspectives, strategies and tactics, developed by the Zapatistas, including the use of cyber disobedience and spread through the networked commons.

Anarchism is composed of, and constructs, networks of autonomous communications. Bey refers to these autonomous networks as "the Web." Despite his use of the conventional terminology of "the Web," Bey is at pains to make clear that what he is speaking of does not refer solely to cyber technology. The information webwork of anarchy, the current forms of the Web, consist of the networks of zines and alternative publications, pirate radios, web sites, listservers, blogs, and hacking. Bey argues (1991, 110) that at this point the Web is primarily a support system capable of sharing information from one autonomous zone to another.

> The networks make up a distinct material infrastructure of communication that uses the technology of mass commercial society—computers, copy machines, mail system —but steers the use of these technologies toward nonprofit, communitarian ends. (Duncombe 1997, 178—179)

The Web provides logistical support for the autonomous zones, but, even more essentially, it also helps bring the autonomous zone into being. In Bey's view the autonomous zone "exists in information-space as well as in the 'real world'" (1991, 109). The Web, in part, makes up for the lack of durability and stability experienced by many autonomous zones. These networks make up the anarchist underground of what Shantz (2008) calls the "future in the present." Its significance rests not in the specifics of technology, but in "the openness and horizontality of the structure" (Bey 1991, 11).

Among anarchists Hakim Bey is at the forefront of efforts recently to develop the political implications of the writings of French philosopher Gilles Deleuze and to bring the insights of these analyses to bear on socio-political practice. Along with critics such as Ronaldo Perez and the Critical Art Ensemble, Bey has attempted a conjoining of Deleuzian analysis with anarchism. One exciting outcome of his adventurous forays into theory is to re-read Proudhonian federalism as Deleuzian rhizome. Here the "non-hegemonic particularities" of federalism express a "nomadological mutuality of synergistic solidarities," the revolutionary structure of opposition to the "one world" of capitalism (1996, 43). For Bey, and other anarchists who have drawn from postmodern theories, this is the structure of revolution and resistance in the contemporary context.

The most exciting result is a provocative and challenging "neo-Proudhonian" rendering of the Zapatista rebellion—one which, unfortunately, is not sufficiently developed. A note of hope is certainly struck: "The goal of 'neo-Proudhonian feder-alism' would be the recognition of freedom at every point of organization in the rhizome, no matter how small A even to a single individual, or any tiny group of 'secessionists'" (1996, 101–102).) Aspects are provided in the understanding of activist nodes in the internet as rhizomatic organizing, of federated cooperation. Several anarchist writers have since attempted to pursue Bey's lead in developing this Deleuzian reading of anarchy and federation.

Despite the best intentions Bey's enthusiasm for revolutionary potentialities (irrespective of sources), as is the case for those who have followed his approach, gets in the way of a searching analysis of the political conditions which make a non-hegemo-nized difference possible (or which encourage instead the trans-formation of difference into the atavistic or xenophobic particu-larisms of ethnic nationalism or religious fundamentalism). His primary response is to hold out the possibility of federation and affinity. Likewise, he overstates the case that these approaches are clearly opposed to capital.

For too long, perhaps, political theorists and activists have been satisfied with dated and worn categories and definitions having as their sole recommendation familiarity. Certainly a critical and extensive re-thinking is overdue. Some (especially Marxists) will feel uneasy with Bey's invitation "to re-read Proudhon, Marx, Nietzsche, Landauer, Fourier, Benjamin, Bakhtin, the IWW, etc. the way the EZLN re-reads Zapata!" (1996, 45). While expressing a distaste for "hyper-intellectual, pyrotechnical writing" and the contemporary vogue of pessimism among cultural theorists, Bey decries what he sees as a reactionary "seduction into inactivity and political despair" (1996, 13). He seeks another way, preferring an "anti-pessimistic" (though not optimistic) politics which seeks the revolutionary potential of humor.

In the end, Bey's discussion itself, like much of the postmodern anarchism that has followed, remains esoteric, of greater interest (and significance) at this point to cultural theorists than to activists seeking strategic assistance in their daily battles against the one world. While such effusions have generally held greater appeal for academic anarchists than for community activists or revolutionaries, Hakim Bey has taken a worthwhile step in renewing socio-political thought by bringing the insights of Deleuzian theory to social action. It appears the journey still has several more miles to go.

While Bey offers an original and innovative, if somewhat esoteric, articulation of anarchy and recent poststructuralist theory, we might suggest that his work continues and extends a thread of everyday anarchism that is a recurrent, if overlooked, presence in earlier waves of anarchist thinking ranging from Kropotkin in the nineteenth century through Gustav Landauer in the early twentieth century to the recent writings of Colin Ward.

The insights of postmodern theory, and their interpretation by contemporary anarchists, are offered at a quite abstract level. Rather than commenting on specific states in specific contexts they are addressed at state forms generally. It is necessary to engage with the specific practices of actual movements and their development through experiences of organizing and struggle. In the following chapter a more grounded approach to anarchism and the defense of the commons is offered—one that builds on histories of anarchist labor organizing, online and off.

Conclusion?

Emphasis must, as always, remain on possibility. This should in no way serve as cause for paralysis. It should remind us that there is no determinism of struggles. The outcome is never assured, rather it must be fought for, or created. At the same time, as anarchists argue, the real potential rests in human creative activity (what another generation might have termed productive activity). This potential is freed up in ways not previously imagined within the communication commons of the networks. A key challenge is to open new venues and vistas for free productive development and interaction—active collaboration. For Summer and Halpin:

> Of course, we cannot know what form this new social system will take. But we should remember that free will and human innovation and creativity are the hidden variables. What may appear to be minor actions can, in these hyper-connected times of critical instability, have consequences magnified beyond imagination. (2010, 120)

Possibilities have shifted, and indeed grown, as decentralized relations in the networks allow for movement beyond the authoritarian and top-down models of political decision-making and action. This in turn allows for the release and circulation of creative involvement that can be impeded within hierarchical and centralized forms. This is the point that anarchists have always made and a key part of their critical analysis of the supposed "democratic centralism" of authoritarian socialism.

Cyber anarchists are pressed to build real, meaningful, connectivity, beyond the vague associations of the internet. This is the challenge addressed in the final chapter.

Chapter 7

Beyond Hacktivism:
Toward Cyber Syndicalism?

The first wave of the alternative globalization movement emerged in large part through new (and newly enabled) connections between movements in the global South and those of the global North in the webworks of the internet. The examples of the Zapatistas found audiences in the activist networks of the global North.

The cyber disobedients used the web in struggle to provide their own news, analysis, and commentary. In events like the protests against the World Trade Organization (WTO) in Seattle in 1999, this allowed them to bypass corporate and state media and produce their own stories about their own actions. It also allowed them to show what the state was doing to people in the streets on a mass scale. All of this aided greatly in developing relations of solidarity, globally as well as locally. For Summer and Halpin:

> As these technologies fall into more and more hands, as is rapidly happening, people who have little at stake in the current social system will use their newfound ability to connect for their own purposes. Collectively, people will be able to react to events much faster than in previous times; and new social order can emerge spontaneously, via the connections people choose to make, rather than order imposed by leaders. (2010, 118)

One might readily look to a range of recent examples from the Arab Spring to Idle No More indigenous resistance in Canada to ongoing alternative globalization movements and various forms of indymedia. These involve expressions, in form if not in name, of anarchy. They express self-organizing practices of the commons.

Floating Signifiers: Into the Ether

Alternative globalization movements in the global North, from their high point in the Quebec City mobilizations against the Free Trade Area of the Americas in 2001 to the present, have been faced with the challenge of rebuilding and finding new ground on which to re-mobilize since the political reaction set in following the 9/11 attacks which derailed momentum and caused many mainstream elements (especially labor unions) to disengage and demobilize (where not playing to the forces of "law and order" reaction). One effect of the post-9/11 freeze (it has been more than a chill) has been the drift away from grounded community (it was never much involved in workplace organizing), outside of some important cases such as indigenous land struggles, as in Ontario and British Columbia, and some direct action anti-poverty movements (like the Ontario Coalition Against Poverty). Instead much organizing has followed certain lines of flight—crucial in the formation of alternative globalization movements from the Seattle protests against the World Trade Organization in 1999—to online activism (in indymedia, hacking, social media, and so on).

In some ways radicalism has continued and developed more consistently, or even fully, online than it has offline in community organizing. Partly, this is an effect of the surveillance apparatus and protest policing that has aggressively targeted "on the ground" movements.

The cyber sphere has provided some spaces for maneuver not available in the streets or in the hood. On the one hand, movement commentators have noted the decline of movements in the period after 9/11 up to the moment of brief resurgence manifested in the Occupy encampments. On the other hand, the cyber disobedients have offered some inspiration and reason for hope. Indeed, the networks of the web have been perhaps uniquely important in allowing for some ongoing activity connecting social movement organizers during the period of decline and dissipation of struggles. Indeed, this is always an important task—maintaining movements through inevitable low periods of struggle and sustaining some capacity for collective re-emergence and revival as possibilities for an uptick of struggles open up. This was perhaps more difficult in periods prior to the development of the web when opportunities for communication, skill sharing, and resource circulation were more limited or localized and when demoralization within face to face circles could finish a movement.

The future potential of movements in struggle will rely in part on the growing convergence, even symbiosis, of the cyber disobedients and the direct actionists of the streets. Even more important will be the grounding of this action and organizing in specific workplaces and neighborhoods in ways that challenge fundamentally relations and structures of ownership, control, and exploitation.

Counterpower

Cyber anarchy represents a real form of counterpower as discussed by autonomist Marxist Antonio Negri. For Negri, a counterpower involves three distinguishable aspects. These are resistance (against the old power); insurrection; and what he calls *potenza*, or that which is constitutive of a new power (or constituent power).

Popular accounts of social struggle tend to focus on the insurrectionary aspects of cyber disobedience, or sometimes (rarely) give a sense that there is resistance being undertaken, but never on the *potenza* of this practice. Never, either, is it hinted at that there is, in fact, a counterpower in play. That is perhaps not too surprising given the hegemonic function of media and state discussions of online activism.

Where insurrection pushes resistance to innovation, *potenza* or constituent power expresses new projects of life. For Negri: "And, whereas the insurrection is a weapon that destroys the life-forms of the enemy, constituent power is the force that positively organizes new schemas of life and mass enjoyment of life" (2008, 140). This is not a replacement of existing power (in the sense of the Leninist workers' state). It is not to take over the reins of the old power. Rather it is to develop new, alternative forms of organization and production—of the commons, of life.

Resistance to the dominant power must be built from the bottom if it is to contribute to the expression of a counterpower. As Negri suggests:

> Resisting it from the bottom means extending and building into the resistance the 'common' networks of knowledge and action, against the privatization of command and wealth. It means breaking the hard of exploitation and exclusion. It means constructing common languages, in which the alternative of a free life and the struggle against death can emerge victorious. (2008, 147)

The building of resistance from the found up and the manifestation of *potenza* requires the development, maintenance, and extension of shared resources and organization. That is, it requires the construction of what Shantz (2010a) has termed infrastructures of resistance. Infrastructures of resistance are those resources that sustain communities in struggle (through food, child care, education, shelter, and so on) while also allowing for the intensification of struggles. In previous periods, important infrastructures of resistance have included union halls, working class newspapers, mutual aid societies, anarchist free schools, and so on. In the present period many of the infrastructures of resistance in poor and working class communities have been destroyed or dissipated after decades of neoliberal assault and the professionalization and legalization of union structures and practices.

The decline of infrastructures of resistance has been accompanied by, and in part caused by, the drift of resistance into "activism," detached from communities of the working class and oppressed. Activism stands as the separation of social and political action into a distinct realm—most typically symbolic street protests—taken up and managed by "activists." The activists tend to be more privileged, at least economically and culturally, having had professional training in post-secondary institutions, and are not necessarily intrinsically connected with the communities they seek to represent or "defend." At the same time they tend to fall back on specific, familiar, activist repertoires to express their dissent (marches, demonstrations, banner drops, and so on). Media savvy their politics are typically symbolic and geared at "awareness raising" or the venting of anger—each geared towards achieving coverage in the media. Protest actions tend to be of a consumerist nature (including against social service agencies) rather than on the basis of directly experienced exploitation in the workplace or labor market.

While this has limited, and in a sense detached and weakened, social struggles, the limitations of such political action (mirrored by the drift of unions into contract management and lobbying) show the need to (re)build infrastructures from the ground up. This includes the tech infrastructures wielded by the cyber disobedients.

Return to the Roots: On Cyber Syndicalism and Workers' Control

In thinking about the context for survival of connectivity and extension of cyber disobedience it is perhaps worthwhile going back to the future, once again. Perhaps too much of cyber activism, and activism in general, has moved online (in hacking, info releases, DOS attacks and so on). One outcome has been a certain loss of connectivity—of the type that connects cyber disobedience with real world material networks in specific contexts of grounded struggle—in workplaces and communities of the working classes and oppressed. Perhaps what is much, if not most, needed is a return to the material context of cyber production (and distribution).

In this there is much to be re/learned by a return to the organizing practices and perspectives of the cyber Wobblies of TAO Communications. Due to the fetishization of the "new," which has become a driving mania of the global cyber age, TAO members sought to embrace something with a bit more history and substance, even if viewed as rather old or passé, the anti-authoritarian revolutionary politics of anarcho-syndicalism, or revolutionary unionism. TAO (a playful acronym for variously The Anarchy Organization or Tasty Apples and Oranges and others; not to be confused with the NSA hacking squad which curiously took the name TAO or Tailored Access Operations, perhaps to mess with activists?) wanted to push against the closing window of the open (non-enclosed) web by opening up sourcecode and access, securing any and all worker-owned and operated access, and cultivating an internationalist network based on mutual aid and sharing rather than profit. TAO workers sought to maintain and defend autonomy and be able thereby to extend support, infrastructure, and relative security to radical communications. As workers, secretaries and coders for student, labor, and environmental groups, the emphasis was placed on social struggle, on bodies in the workplaces, communities, and streets, rather than so-called "virtual" reality. TAO traveling organizers denied the internet's very existence (as a mythologized space free from labor and class), and spoke instead about ownership of the means of production, about boots on the ground, gardens on rooftops, and other such sticky aspects of old-fashioned materiality.

Several projects were initiated or taken forward to secure gains in struggle. Among the most important or durable, of the online efforts, has perhaps been A-Infos. A-Infos was a mailing list gleaned from various paper addresses the Toronto publication *Anarchives* had gathered since the 1960s, joined with the e-list established by the I-AFD in Europe, and supported by Freedom Press, which has operated out of London since Kropotkin and others started it in the 1880s. A-Infos came to be carried on its own server, and its multiple lists and digests distribute news "by, for, and about" anarchists to over 1200 subscribers in at least 12 languages, with substantial daily traffic, as well as print and radio reproduction around the world. A-Infos became the most important daily news source on anarchist activities. It has been crucial in posting anarchist calls for participation in various struggles continuing to today.

Other projects supported by TAO with more or less success include: The Student Activist Network, the Direct Action Media Network (an unfortunately defunct precursor to the Indymedia conglomerate), PIRG.CA (public interest research groups in the Canadian context). Solidarity projects included work with the Ontario Coalition Against Poverty, Esgenoopetitj (colonial name: Burnt Church) First Nations, CUPE 3903 (teaching assistants at York University, during a historic strike won in 2001), and numerous groups formed to oppose imperialist wars after September 11. From the original single machine, TAO came to operate at least eight boxes, serving the needs of more than 1000 members, a spread of organizations and individuals, who self-manage thousands of lists, hundreds of web pages, as well as databases. Besides basic shell access without advertisements or space quotas, organized TAO workers have provided secure access to web-based e-mail, secure online communications, and more.

In 1999 TAO workers joined the Industrial Workers of the

World (IWW) with the intention of forming a branch amongst telecom workers in the Toronto area. It was believed that this would solidify syndicalist and co-operative structures, help with the rotation of job tasks, improve benefits for TAO workers, and generally raise class consciousness, particularly in the on-line arena where labor is too often made invisible and victimized by speed need.

TAO members, crucially, saw themselves first and foremost as tech workers involved in a specific, if shifting, mode of production, wielding specific means of production, and connected through particular relations of production. Their impetus was a primal (rather than neo) one. It was the impetus of the worker struggling to overcome exploitation, gain or maintain control of one's production, and determine the nature of their work (and livelihood), and the conditions of their communities.

Many info activists loosely affiliated or in co-operation with the original Toronto TAO collective went on to form other locals and collectives (in Montreal, Vancouver, Edmonton, New York City, Seattle) as well as Indymedia formations. This includes one of the biggest on Turtle Island, Riseup (riseup.net) which continues to organize. Riseup "birds" work collectively maintaining "riseup networks" and developing code in "riseup labs." Riseup runs more than 10,000 mailing lists. There is also a lively current operation, Koumbit, run by a self-managed "Council of Workers." The ECN (European Counter Networks) are very broad networks run by the collectives called "Isole Nella Rete" (Italian, "Islands in the Net"). They are engaged in solid antifascist and migrant defense work.

The most significant possibilities of cyber disobedience do not rest with direct action hits on state or corporate targets. There is a potential for real power in the collective actions of hacktivists as tech workers directly, and collectively, at the point of production, as TAO workers suggested almost at the beginning of the popular web. During times of a strike of tech workers everyone can see whose labor makes the wi-fi and Internet possible. When that labor is withdrawn the system literally goes offline. With growing areas of states and capital entirely dependent on cyber infrastructures, any collective action by tech workers can have a dramatic impact, threatening the basis of command and profit and starkly posing questions of ownership and control.

Even more than collective strike actions, hacktivists can contribute to the remaking of tech resources for purposes that serve a tech (and social) commons As Squire suggests:

> The potential, though, does not end with bringing IT systems down. Their role as the experts in the configuration and use of IT infrastructure also means that IT workers, organized as part of the working class, have the potential to reshape some of the existing IT infrastructure so that it can be used by, for and in the interests of the working class as a whole – removing copyright restrictions on online data or remodeling for-profit websites so that they are freely accessible to everyone, for example. IT workers can play a role in reclaiming the online commons. (2013, n.p.)

As TAO members argued more than a decade ago, hacktivists must come to see themselves as tech workers who have specific skills that can be used, not only reactively or as activists, but also constructively and productively. This is a constructive anarchy involved in the building of infrastructures of resistance (Shantz 2010a). The possibilities for organizing on a class basis as tech workers over issues of exploitation and control of labor may expand as tech work becomes more and more deskilled and/or devalued. This is an ongoing process of what some commentators refer to as the "proletarianization" of tech work (Squire 2013).

The possibilities for a better alternative emerging—in place of the authoritarian forms of what might coalesce as neo-fascism or prison-industrial capitalism—are dependent upon rooted material forms of organization and the preparatory building of the infrastructures of resistance. Tools and practices of cyber disobedience will be important parts in the day-to-day work of these infrastructures of resistance and in their construction, but they are not a substitute for the organizations, resources, and relationships that make up infrastructures of resistance themselves. This is what the early TAO organizers understood clearly, but which many later generations of cyber activists have lost track of.

Cyber anarchists, and activists more broadly, need to devote more attention to affirming what they want—what they are for rather than what they are against—and preparing conditions, providing means, by which it might be realized. Direct action in tech workplaces, and organized efforts toward workers' control can secure these means—indeed, they will not be secured without syndicalist organizing in tech industries.

Endnotes

Chapter 3

1. Mansfield-Devine S. DDoS: threats and mitigation. Network Security [serial - online]. -December 1, 2011; 2011(12): 5-12. Available from: E-Journals, Ipswich, MA. Accessed March 25, 2012.

2. Hacktivism: coined by Omega, a hacker, and member of the Cult of the Dead Cow in 1998. The term refers to the combination of computer hacking and political activism. (http://www.wired.com/techbiz/it/news/2004/07/64193." Wired News, July 14, 2004. Retrieved March 10, 2012.)

3. "http://www.nytimes.com/2009/06/16/books/16situation. html?_r=1." New York Times, June 15, 2009. Retrieved March 10, 2012.

4. Ibid, P. 16

5. The Communist Manifesto, Karl Marx and Friedrich Engels, P. 70

6. http://news.cnet.com/8301-31921_3-20062398-281.html CNET. May 12, 2011. Retrieved March 11, 2012.

7. Free sharing of technological information.

8. Note: The proposed SOPA & PIPA bills are similar reflection to the English Enclosure Acts proposed by the Feudal lords when wealth was needed. In the same way that they expropriated land, passed laws that legalized the theft of land and created enclosures of the "commons." The Internet is now becoming privatized. In the feudal period, the laws and enclosure acts were enforced by the military; today, we are seeing the same occurrence with Homeland Security, FBI, RCMP, and CSIS. The theft of the "commons," or in today's terms the Internet as a commune; the acts are being upheld through law and force. The intellectual theft of property and software piracy is being done under the conditions of capitalist competition; individual capitalists are acting on

their self-interests of "profit" or exploitation. The work being done by criminal justice agencies may be for the best interests of their company, and the state police appear to be there to referee that competition. As a result, accessibility to information is taken back.

9. English Wikipedia anti-SOPA Blackout, January 18, 2012. Retrieved March 11, 2012.

10. International Business, Times. "Anonymous Unleashes DDoS Attacks on DOJ, U.S Copyright Office, RIAA, MPAA and Universal Music Sites." *International Business Times 1: Regional Business News*. Web. 27 March. 2012.

11. http://www.wired.com/gamelife/2011/05/sony-online-enter-tainment-hack/ *WIRED*.
May 2, 2011. Retrieved March 12, 2012.

12. This quote is a reference to the 1982 book "V for Vendetta"; Anonymous members also often quote the 2005 film adaptation and wear Guy Fawkes masks as made popular through Occupy movements protesting against tyranny, politicians and corporations.

13. Geers, Kenneth. "The Cyber Threat To National Critical Infrastructures: Beyond Theory." *Journal Of Digital Forensic Practice 3*.2-4 (2010): 124-130. E Journals. Web. 28 March. 2012.

14. www.stratfor.com

15. Where an estimated 86-145 Afghani's were killed, mostly children, by an American aircraft on May 4th, 2009.

16. A satirical term coined by Stephen Colbert referring to telling truths from "the gut" without regard to evidence or logic.

17. *The Communist Manifesto*, Karl Marx and Friedrich Engels, P. 40

Chapter 4

1. Zero-day vulnerability: a vulnerability whose details are unknown. Its exploitation can potentially yield any privilege on the destination host. (Wang et al., 2010)

2. Phishing: a form of social engineering in which an attacker attempts to fraudulently acquire sensitive information from a victim by impersonating a trustworthy third party. (Jagatic et al., 2005, p. 1)

References

Adefurin, A. 2011. "Ciprofloxacin Safety in Pediatrics: A Systematic Review." *Archives of Disease in Childhood.*

Agnew, R. 1992. "Foundation for a General Strain Theory." *Criminology* 30(1): 47–87.

"Anarchist Violence as Acts of War." *Huffington Post.* April 26. http://www.huffingtonpost.com/steven-kurlander/a-lesson-of-the-boston-bombings_b_3156494.html

Anonymous. 2012. http://www.anonpaste.me/anonpaste/index.php?23a693 bafc9b3cbd#EKwY3Tvnge77IokYzy4GmSKj8a2mrP3Jp0Vanh MaeuI= Accessed Nov 19, 2012.

Babbie, E. 2003. *The Practice of Social Research*, 10th edition. Wadsworth: Thomson Learning Inc.

Badiou, Alain. 2011. *Polemics.* London: Verso.

Beck, J. 1999. "The False Claims Act and the English Eradication of Qui Tam Legislation." *North Carolina Law Review* 78(3): 539–642.

Beck, U. 2000. "The Cosmopolitan Perspective: Sociology of the Second Age of Modernity." *British Journal of Sociology* 51: 79–105.

Bey, Hakim. 1996. *Millenium.* New York: Autonomedia.

— — —. 1991. *Immediatism.* San Francisco: AK Press.

Biderman, A. and A. Reiss. 1967. "On Exploring the 'Dark Figure' of Crime." *The Annals of the American Academy of Political and Social Science* 374: 1–15.

Brito, J. 2011. "'We Do It for the Lulz': What Makes LulzSec Tick?" June 17. *Time Magazine,* Computers, http://techland.time.com/2011/06/17/we-do-it-for-the-lulz-what-makes-lulzsec-tick/ Accessed July 26, 2012.

Bucket, D. 2004. "Scientist Gets Congratulatory Letter from Health Canada After Being Fired." *Canadian Press, News*

August 4.

http://www.healthcoalition.ca/archive/yourfired.pdf Accessed November 18, 2012.

Burleigh, Michael. 2010. *Blood and Rage: A Cultural History of Terrorism.* New York: Harper.

Callender, C. 2010. "Stephen Hawking Says There's no Theory of Everything." *CultureLab* http://www.newscientist.com/blogs/culturelab/2010/09/ stephen-hawking-says-theres-no-theory-of-everything.html

Chesterton, G.K. 2008 [1907]. *The Man who was Thursday: A Nightmare.* London: Penguin.

Cleaver, Harry. 1992. "Kropotkin, Self-valorization and the Crisis of Marxism." Paper presented at the Conference on Pyotr Alexeevich Kropotkin, Russian Academy of Science, Moscow, St. Petersburg, and Dimitrov, December 8–14.

Clippinger, John and David Bollier. 2005. "A Renaissance of the Commons: How the New Sciences and Internet Are Framing a New Global Identity and Order." In *CODE: Collaborative Ownership and the Digital Economy,* ed. Rishab Aiyer Ghosh. Boston: MIT Press.

CNET. 2011. http://news.cnet.com/8301-31921_3-20062398-281. html *CNET* May 12. Accessed March 11, 2012.

Cohen, N. 2010. "Iraq Video Brings Notice to a Web Site." *New York Times, World,*April 6. *http://www.nytimes.com/2010/04/07/world/07wikileaks.html* Accessed November 7, 2012.

Coleman, Gabriella. 2012a. *Coding Freedom: The Ethics and Aesthetics of Hacking.* Princeton University Press.

Conrad, Joseph. 1963 [1907]. *The Secret Agent.* London: Penguin.

———. 2012b. "Everything You Know about Anonymous is Wrong." http://www.aljazeera.com/indepth/opinion/2012/05/ 201255152158991826.html

Deibert, Ronald. 2013. "Metadata." *The Globe and Mail*. Tuesday, June 11, A11.

Dodd, G. 2008. "'Anonymous' Hackers Vow to 'Dismantle' Scientology." *Xinhuanet*, January 25. http://news.xinhuanet.com/english/200801/25/content_7495986.htm Accessed July 24, 2012.

Doherty, Brian. 2012. "What 3-D Printing Means for Gun Rights." *Reason*. http://reason.com/archives/2012/12/12/what-3-d-printing-means-for-gun-rights

Duncombe, Stephen. 1997. *Notes from Underground: Zines and the Politics of Alternative Culture*. London: Verso.

Felson, M. 2006. *Crime and Nature*. Thousand Oaks, CA: Sage.

Foreign Intelligence Surveillance Court. 2013. "United States Foreign Intelligence Surveillance Court." *Washington, D.C.* Docket Number: BR 13–80.

Foster, John Bellamy and Robert McChesney. 2011. "The Internet's Unholy Marriage to Capitalism." *Monthly Review*. 62(10). http://monthlyreview.org/2011/03/01/the-internets-unholy-marriage-to-capitalism

Foucault, M. 1976. *The History of Sexuality*. London: Penguin.

— — —. 1977. *Discipline & Punishment: The Birth of the Prison*. New York: Vintage Books.

— — —. 1978. "Spaces of Security: The Example of the Town." *Political Geography* 26: 48–56.

— — —. 1982. "The Subject and Power." *Critical Inquiry* 8(4): 777–795.

— — —. 1998. *Ethics: Subjectivity and Truth (Essential Works of Foucault, 1954-1984)*. Ed. P. Rabinow. New York: New Press.

Freeze, Colin and Josh Wingrove. 2013. "Opposition, Privacy Watchdog Question Surveillance Program." *The Globe and Mail*. Tuesday, June 11, A1.

Frum, David. 2013. "The Internet's Do-It-Yourself Culture, Gone Deadly." *National Post*. Saturday, May 11.

http://fullcomment.nationalpost.com/2013/05/11/david-frum-2/

Gallagher, S. 2012. "'Patriotic Hacktivist' The Jester Unmasked — Or Maybe It's a Big Troll." *ARS Technica,* Cyberwar. May 15. http://arstechnica.com/security/2012/05/patriotic-hacktivist-the-jester-unmasked-or-maybe-its-a-big-troll/ Accessed July 25, 2012.

Geers, Kenneth. 2010. "The Cyber Threat To National Critical Infrastructures: Beyond Theory." *Journal Of Digital Forensic Practice* 3(2–4): 124–130. E Journals. Web. March 28, 2012.

Gill, N. 2012. "Assange Says U.S. Wikileaks Inquiry Reveals His Life's at Risk." *Bloomberg Businessweek, News,* September 27. *http://www.businessweek.com/news/2012-09-27/assange-says-u-dot-s-dot-wikileaks-inquiry-reveals-his-life-s-at-risk* (accessed on November 14, 2012).

Globe and Mail, The. 2013. "For Parliament, not a Minister Alone." *The Globe and Mail.* Tuesday, June 11, A16.

Goldberg, L. (Producer), and J. Badham (Director). 1983. *WarGames.* United States: MGM/UA Entertainment Company.

Gonzalez, J. 2012. "$104M Payday from to IRS for UBS Whistleblower." *NY Daily News* September 12. *http://articles.nydailynews.com/2012-09-12/news/33768861 _1_bradley-birkenfeld-money-in-swiss-banks-tax-fraud* Accessed November 19, 2012.

Gramsci, A. 1971. *Selections from the Prison Notebooks.* Ed. Q. Hoare and G. Smith. New York: International Publishers.

Gunkel D. 2005. "Editorial: Introduction to Hacking and Hacktivism." *New Media Society* 7(5): 595–597.

Hacker. 2011. *In Merriam-Webster.com.* Retrieved July 20, 2012, from http://www.merriam-webster.com/dictionary/hacker

Hesse-Biber, S. N. and P. Leavy. 2011. *The Practice of Qualitative Research,* 2nd edition. London: Sage Publications.

Hay, D. 1975. "Property, Authority and the Criminal Law," In

Albion's Fatal Tree: Crime and Society in Eighteenth-Century England, ed. D. Hay, P. Linebaugh, J. G. Rule, E. P. Thompson, and C. Winslow. New York: Pantheon.

Hirschi, T. 1969. *Causes of Delinquency*. Berkeley: University of California Press.

Hong, Nathaniel. 1992. "Constructing the Anarchist Beast in American Periodical Literature, 1880-1903." Critical Studies in Mass Communication 9: 110–130.

H.R.3261. "Stop Online Piracy Act" (Introduced in House – IH).

Hui, Sylvia. 2013. "LOL No More: Four Hackers Sent to Prison." *National Post*. Friday, May 17, A14.

International Business, Times. "Anonymous Unleashes DDoS Attacks on DOJ, U.S Copyright Office, RIAA, MPAA and Universal Music Sites." *International Business Times* 1: Regional Business News. Web. March 27, 2012.

Invisible Committee, The. 2007. *The Coming Insurrection*. France: La Fabrique.

Invisible Committee, The. 2008. *The Coming Insurrection*. New York: Semiotext(e).

ITU World Telecommunication. 2011. "ICT Facts and Figures." http://www.itu.int/ITUD/ict/facts/2011/material/ICTFacts Figures2011.pdf Accessed November 18, 2012.

Jagatic, T., N. Johnson, M. Jakobsson, and F. Menczer. 2005. *Social Phishing*. Indian University, Bloomington, 1–10.

James, Henry. 1977 [1886]. *The Princess Casamassima*. London: Penguin.

Jordan, T. and P. Taylor. 1998. "A Sociology of Hackers." *The Sociological Review* 46(4): 757–780.

Kernaghan, K. and J. Langford. 1990. *The Responsible Public Servant*. Halifax: Institute for Research on Public Policy.

Kernaghan, K. 2003. "The Future Role of a Professional, Non-Partisan Public Service in Ontario." Panel on the Role of Government, Research Paper Series No. 13.

Kline, Jesse. 2013. "Three Cheers for the Printed Gun." *National*

Post. Friday, May 17, A12.

Kocieniewski, D. 2012. "Whistle-Blower Awarded $104 Million by I.R.S." *New York Times, Business* September 11. *http://www.nytimes.com/2012/09/12/business/whistle-blower-awarded-104-million-by-irs.html?_r=0* Accessed November 18, 2012.

Kohn, S., M. Kohn, and D. Colapinto. 2004. *Whistleblower Law: A Guide to Legal Protections for Corporate Employees.* Westport: Praeger Publishers.

Kovac, E. 2012. "Anonymous to Launch TYLER, Wikileaks on Steroids." *Softpedia, News,* March 3. *http://news.softpedia.com/news/Anonymous-to-Launch-TYLER-WikiLeaks-on-Steroids-267533.shtml* Accessed November 14, 2012.

Kravets, D. 2012. "Wikileaks Goes Behind Paywall, Anonymous Cries Foul." *Wired* October 11. *http://www.wired.com/threatlevel/2012/10/wikileaks-paywall-anonymous/* Accessed November 17, 2012.

Kurlander, Steven. 2013. "A Lesson of the Boston Bombings: Stop Classifying Criminal.

Lahman, L. 2005 "Bad Mules: A Primer on the Federal False Claims Act."

Lakhani, K. and R. Wolf. 2003. "Why Hackers Do What They Do: Understanding Motivation Effort in Free/Open Source Software Projects." *The Boston Consulting Group* 1–28.

Lee, M. and B. Campbell. 2006. "Putting Canadians at Risk: How the Federal Government's Deregulation Agenda Threatens Health and Environment Standards." *Canadian Center for Policy Initiatives.*

Ludlow, Peter (ed.). 2001. *Crypto Anarchy, Cyberstates, and Pirate Utopias.* Boston: Bradford.

Mansfield-Devine S. 2011. "DDoS: Threats and Mitigation." *Network Security* 12: 5-12. Accessed March 25, 2012.

Mathiason, N. 2001. "Blowing the Final Whistle." *The Observer, News* November 24.

http://www.guardian.co.uk/business/2001/nov/25/businessofresearch.research Accessed November 18, 2012.

McLuhan, M. 1962. *The Gutenberg Galaxy: The Making of Typographic Man.* Toronto: University of Toronto Press.

Mehta, D. and E. Darier. 1997. "Virtual Control and Disciplining on the Internet: Electronic Governmentality in the New Wired World." *The Information Society* 14: 107–116.

Méndez, J. 2012. "Report of the Special Rapporteur on Torture and Other Cruel, Inhuman or Degrading Treatment or Punishment." United Nations General Assembly.

Merriman, John. 2009. *The Dynamite Club: How a Bombing in Fin-de-Siècle Paris Ignited the Age of Modern Terror.* New York: Houghton Mifflin Harcourt.

Milevski, L. 2011. "Stuxnet and Strategy: A Special Operation in Cyberspace?" *Joint Force Quarterly* 63: 64–69.

Miller, J. 2000. *The Passion of Michel Foucault.* Massachusetts: Harvard University Press.

Miller, Scott. 2011. *The President and the Assassin: McKinley, Terror and Empire at the Dawn of the American Century.* New York: Random House

Mlot, S. 2012. "Anonymous Targets Pedophiles Via #OpPedoChat Campaign." *PC May,* July 11. http://www.pcmag.com/article2/0,2817,2406981,00.asp Accessed July 26, 2012.

Moffitt, T. 1993. "Adolescent-Limited and Life-Course Persistent Antisocial Behavior: A Developmental Taxonomy." *Psychological Review* 100: 674–701.

Montjoye, Y., C. Hidalgo, M. Verleysen, and V. Blondel. 2013. "Unique in the Crowd: The Privacy Bounds of Human Mobility." *Scientific Reports* 3: 1376.

Moore, R. 2005. *Cybercrime: Investigating High Technology Computer Crime,* 2nd edition. Cincinnati, OH: Anderson Publishing Company.

National Crime Records Bureau. 2009. "Cybercrimes."

http://ncrb.nic.in/CII%202009/cii-2009/Chapter%2018.pdf

Near, J. and M. Miceli. 1985. "Organizational Dissidence: The Case of Whistle-Blowing." *Journal of Business Ethics* 4: 1–16.

Negri, Antonio. 2008. *Reflections on Empire*. London: Polity.

Neumann, P. 2004. "Principled Assuredly Trustworthy Composable Systems and Networks." *Compute Science Lab* 1–174.

Newman, O. 1972. *Defensible Space*. New York: Macmillan..

New York Times. 2009. "http://www.nytimes.com/2009/06/16/books/16situation.html?_r=1." *New York Times* June 15. Accessed March 10, 2012.

Nikitina, S. 2012. "Hackers as Tricksters of the Digital Age." *Journal of Popular Culture* 45(1): 133–152.

Olsen, P. 2012. *We are Anonymous*. New York: NY: Little, Brown and Company.

Oxblood Ruffin. 2004. "Hacktivism, from Here to There." http://www.cultdeadcow.com/cDc_files/cDc-0384.php

Pavlich, G. 2011. *Law & Society*. London: Oxford University Press.

Peyser, M. (Producer) and I. Softley. (Director). 1995. *Hackers*. United States: United Artists.

Plato. 2012. *The Republic*. London: Penguin.

Rauchway, Eric. 2004. *Murdering McKinley: The Making of Theodore Roosevelt's America*. New York: Hill and Wang.

Reinharz, S. 1992. *Feminist Methods in Social Research*. New York: Oxford University Press.

Rongine, N.M. 1985. "Toward a Coherent Legal Response to the Public Policy Dilemma Posed by Whistleblowing." *American Business Law Journal* 23(2): 23–28.

RT. 2012. "Anonymous Warns Israel: 'No One Cuts Internet on our Watch.'" November 15. http://rt.com/news/gaza-israel-strike-anonymous-787/ Accessed Nov 19, 2012.

Schwartz, M. 2012a. "Anonymous Hands Wikileaks 2.4 Million Syrian Emails." *Information Week,* Security, July 10.

http://www.informationweek.com/news/security/attacks /240003443 Accessed July 23, 2012.

Schwartz, M. 2012b. "Who is Anonymous: 10 Key Facts." *Information Week* February 2. http://www.informationweek.com/security/attacks/who-is-anonymous-10-key-facts/232600322 Accessed November 12, 2012.

Shantz, Jeff. 2012. *Protest and Punishment: Repression and Resistance in the Era of Neoliberal Globalization*. Durham: Carolina Academic Press.

———. 2010a. *Constructive Anarchy: Building Infrastructures of Resistance*. Surrey: Ashgate.

———. 2010b. "Policing Protest." *Linchpin*. http://linchpin.ca/?q=content/policing-protest

———. 2008. "Anarchist Futures in the Present." *Resistance Studies* 1(1), http://rsmag.nfshost.com/wp-content/uploads/anarchistfu-tures200801.html

Silver, J. (Producer) and J. McTeigue (Director). (2005). *V for Vendetta*. United States: Warner Brothers Pictures.

Silver, J. (Producer) and D. Sena (Director). (2001). *Swordfish*. United States: WarnerBrothers Pictures.

Skogan, W. 1977. "Dimensions of the Dark Figure of Unreported Crime." *Crime & Delinquency* 43: 41–50.

Slevin, Carl. 2003. "Anarchism." *The Concise Oxford Dictionary of Politics*. Ed. Iain McLean and Alistair McMillan. Oxford: Oxford University Press.

Smith, N. and P. Gabela. 1974. "Job Security for Public Employees." *Law Journal Library*.

Solyom, C. 2012. "Anonymous: Commander X Speaks Out (With Video)." *The Montreal Gazette*, News, May 13. http://www.montrealgazette.com/news/Anonymous+Commander+speaks+with+video/668583/story.html (accessed on July 30, 2012).

Spiegel. 2010. "The Wikileaks Iraq War Logs." *Spiegel Online, International, World* October 22. *http://www.spiegel.de/international/world/the-wikileaks-iraq-war-logs-greatest-data-leak-in-us-military-history-a-724845.html* Accessed November 16, 2012.

Squire, Jo. 2013. "Anonymous and the Future of Hacktivism." *Socialist Alternative* 27. http://sa.org.au/index.php?option=com_k2&view=item&id =7760:anonymous-and-the-future-of-hacktivism&Itemid=543

Stryker, C. 2011. "Anonymous Attacks Westboro Baptist Church After All, Takes Down WBC Website." *Urlesque,* Main, February 24. http://www.urlesque.com/2011/02/24/anonymous-westboro-baptist-churchattack/ Accessed July 24, 2012.

Summer, Kay and Harry Halpin. 2010. "The Crazy before the New." In *What Would it Mean to Win?,* eds. Turbulence Collective. Oakland: PM Press, 113–120.

Taylor, M. 1982. *Community, Anarchy and Liberty.* Cambridge, England: Cambridge University Press.

Taylor, P. 1999. *Hackers: Crime in the Digital Sublime.* London: Routledge.

Thomas, P. 2005. "Debating a Whistle-Blower Protection Act for Employees of the Government of Canada." *Canadian Public Administration.*

Toews, Vic. 2012. "In Canada. Parliament. House of Commons." *Debates.* 41st Parliament, 1st Session. March 27. Ottawa: Canadian Government Publishing.

Tomblin, J. and G. Jenion, G. (forthcoming). "Sentencing 'Anonymous': Exacerbating the Civil Divide between Online Citizens and Government."

Turgeman-Goldschmidt, O. 2005. "Hackers' Accounts: Hacking as Social Entertainment." *Social Science Computer Review* 23(8): 8–23.

Waites, R. 2011. "V for Vendetta Masks: Who's Behind Them?

BBC News, October 20.
http://www.bbc.co.uk/news/magazine-15359735 (accessed on July 23, 2012).

Wang, L., A. Singhal, S. Jajodia, and S.Noel. 2010. "*K*-Zero Day Safety: Measuring the Security Risk of Networks against Unknown Attacks." *European Symposium on Research in Computer Security (E)*.

Warren, H.S. 2003. *Hacker's Delight*. Boston, MA: Addison-Wesley Professional.

Williams, C. 2011. "Anonymous 'Robin Hood' Hacking Attack Hits Major Firms." *The Telegraph*, Technology, December 28. http://www.telegraph.co.uk/technology/news/8980453/Anony mous-Robin-Hood-hacking-attack-hits-major-firms.html (accessed on July 26, 2012).

Williams, C. 2012. "Barack Obama 'Ordered Stuxnet Cyber Attacks on Iran.'" *The Telegraph, News* http://www.telegraph.co.uk/technology/news/9305704/ Barack-Obama-ordered-Stuxnet-cyber-attack-on-Iran.html

Wing, P. 1998. "White-Hat Hackers." *Data Communications* 27(4): 1–31.

WIRED. 2011. "http://www.wired.com/gamelife/2011/05/sony-online-enter-tainment-hack/" *WIRED* May 2. Accessed March 12, 2012.

Wired News. 2004. "http://www.wired.com/techbiz/it/news/2004/07/64193." *Wired News* July 14. Accessed March 10, 2012.

Wolak, J., K. Mitchell, and D. Finkelhor. 2007. "Does Online Harassment Constitute Bullying? An Exploration of Online Harassment by Known Peers and Online-Only Contacts." Journal of Adolescent Health 41(6), S51–S58.

Žižek, Slavoj. 1998. "Psychoanalysis and Post-Marxism: The Case of Alain Badiou." *The South Atlantic Quarterly* 97(2): 235–261. http://www.lacan.com/zizek-badiou.htm

Index

3D printing, 10–15
9/11, 36, 37, 128

A
A-Infos (anarchist news
  service), 133
academia, 38, 81
activism
Anonymous and, 98
as privileged, detached, representational, 131
See also cyber-disobedience,
  hacktivism
Age of Information, Age of
  Awakened, 41, 61, 69, 70, 72,
  76, 87, 103
Agnew, Robert, 45
anarchism , anarchy
  criminalization of, 21, 24–25,
    38
  cyber, 14, 20, 107–8, 111
  etymology, definitions of, 9
  literary (mis)representations
    of, 28–33
  resurgence of, 22
  techno-, 11
anarchist(s) , 9–10
  A-Infos, 133
  production, 35
  state, police and, 12, 15, 21,
    23

syndicalism, 132–34, 136. *See
  also* syndicalism
  theoretical approaches by, 45
  See also TAO
anonymity , 6
  crime and intrusions, 79
  technologies that enable, 79
Anonymous, 5–8
  anarchist, revolutionary
    philosophies of, 49, 59, 61
  as an idea, not a group,
    71–74
  as loose hacktivist 'group,'
    41–42, 61
  as movement against enclo-
    sures, 104
  formed "for the lulz," 54
  relationship to Wikileaks,
    100–101
anti-civilization, 113–114
anti-technology, 113–114
Arab Spring, 4, 5, 6, 14, 122
art, 38 , 59, 123
assassinations, 24, 25, 32
Assange, Julian, 91, 94, 100,
  101
authoritarianism, 114–15
  control over minds and
    bodies, 10
autonomy, 110

B

Badiou, Alain, 35, 36, 37, 117

Bakunin, Mikhail, 37

Barbrook, Richard , 1

Beck, Ulrich, 34, 78, 94

Benjamin, Walter, 120

Bey, Hakim, 117–24

big data, 17

bit torrent. *See also* P2P, 11

black bloc, 23

bombings,

historical, 24–25, 33, 38. *See also* *the* Unabomber

in film, 57

in literature, 29

C

Canada

Bill C-30 'Protecting Children from Internet Predators Act,' 84–85

CSIS (Can. Security & Intelligence Services) and CSEC, 16–17

metadata surveillance in, 15–18

state repression in, 19, 36

whistleblowing in, 87, 90–93, 103

capitalism

conflicts with commons, 106–9, 119

free market, 111

infrastructures of resistance to, 135

threats to, 73

censorship, 6, 12, 15, 54, 73

Chesterton, G.K.

The Man Who Was Friday, 28–29

Chopra, Shiv (whistleblower on Health Canada), 91–93

civil disobedience, 4–5, 19–20, 98

Clastres, Pierre, 120

Coleman, Gabriella, 7, 9, 99

Coming Insurrection, The (The Invisible Committee), 62, 63, 65

commodification

processes of, 2–3

conflicts with commons, 106, 109

commonism , 1, 104–5

commons

communication, 2, 3, 10–11, 13, 14, 21

creative, 'open cultures' movements, 12, 107

ecological, social and communications, 105–109

feudalist enclosures of land, 2, 3, 73, 92, 104 , 137n8

modern renaissance of, 104

reclamations of, 3

communes, 63

Paris Commune, 1871, 24

communism , 35, 63, 73, 105

communist(s)
  Soviet and Stalinist regimes,
  22 , 105
  See also Red Scares
complex systems theory,
  111–113
content analysis (research
  methods), 44–45
cooperation , 107–8
  in FOSS and P2P, 110
copyright
  battles over, 65–67, 135
  and 3D printing, 12
corporations
  enclosure of internet, 2
  whistleblowing in/against,
  89–90
crime
  innovation in, 86
  social determinants shaping,
  79, 87
Critical Art Ensemble, 123
cyber disobedience
  and direct action, 5
  introduction to, 2–7
cybercrime
  regulation, discipline,
  governmentality over, 80–85

D
data retention
commodification and, 2–4, 16
  ISP logging, governmen-
  tality, 17–18, 84

See also metadata
decentralization, 115
  of disciplinary power online,
  80
Defense Distributed (3D gun
  print plans), 10–15
Deleuze, Gilles, 123, 124
denial of service attacks,
  distributed (DOS or DDOS),
  4, 13–14, 61, 64, 78–79
desire, 120
deviance, deviants
  authoritarian constructions
  of anarchists as, 24
  crime and, 79, 86
  elite, corporate espionage, 92
  hacker depictions as, 44, 47,
  60
Diebert, Ronald, 16, 17
Diggers or Ranters, 3, 104
direct action, 3, 5, 38, 128–29,
  134–35, 136
  cyberdisobedience and, 5, 20
disciplinary power, 80–86
DIY, do-it-yourself, 11, 35 ,
  108–9, 115, 120
  See also peer-to-peer, 109
Doherty, Brian , 11
Dyer-Witheford, Nick, 105,
  106–7, 109–10, 111, 116

E
Electronic Frontier
  Foundation, 64

elite (power, deviance of), 18,
92
enclosures, 35–36, 111
    corporate net commodifi-
    cation processes, 2–3
    current organising against,
    12, 105, 109, 118, 119
    feudal, of common land, 2,
    94, 104
    statist, 108
encryption , 6, 12–13, 101, 79
ethics , 85, 91, 98, 102
    of hacking, 41–43, 46–47, 53,
    60
    See also whistleblowing
European Counter Networks
    (ecn.net), 134
EZLN. *See* Zapatistas

F
Facebook, 15, 66, 82, 99. *See
    also* the Panopticon
fascism
    neo- or prison-industrial
    capitalism, 135–36
    technological surveillance,
    command and control,
    114–15
FBI (US Federal Bureau of
    Investigations) , 55, 68
feudalism, 2, 73, 92, 104 , 137n8
Foster, John Bellamy, 1, 2–3
Foucault, Michel, (Foucaldian
    theory), 75, 80, 85

G
gaming, video, 12
    See also Playstation hack ;
    WarGames (film)
Gardner, Sue (Wikipedia
    Foundation), 66
globalization, 27 , 76
    alternative or anti-, 19, 20, 26,
    71, 115, 122, 127–28
Global Positioning System. *See*
    GPS
Google, 15, 17, 44
governmentality, 78, 80–85
GPS (Global Positioning
    System), 83
guns , 3D printing of, 11, 14–15

H
hackers
    as workers. *See also* syndi-
    calism, 134–36
    definitions of, 41–43
    ethics of, 41–43, 46–47, 53, 60
    film portrayals of, 43–52
    motivations of, 50, 56–57
    UK prosecutions against, 13
    See also Anonymous
Hackers (film by Iain Softley)
    hacktivism, 41–42
    as reclaiming commons, 135
    described, 4
    etymology of, 63–64
    moral panics around, 38–39
    social or political, 52–53,

71–72
HBGary hack, 68
Health Canada
   unsafe drug approvals, 92
horizontalism, 8, 35, 115 , 122
human rights, 64, 79 , 91

I
immediatism, 117–18
Indigenous peoples,
   movements of, 115, 127, 128,
   133
indignants, 59
Industrial Workers of the
   World (IWW), 26, 133–34
aka. 'Wobblies,' 132
infrastructures of resistance,
   130–31, 136
information
   Age of, 41, 59, 61, 69, 70, 72,
   76, 87, 103
   'wants to be free,' 11, 13 , 98,
   100
insurrection, 24, 49, 57, 98, 121,
   129–30
Invisible Committee, The
   The Coming Insurrection,
   62–63 , 65
Iraq War Logs (US military
   leak), 69, 95
Isole Nella Rete, 134

J
James, Henry, 27–33

K
Kaczynski, Ted. *See*
   Unabomber
Kline, Jesse, 12, 13
Kropotkin, Peter, 30, 133

L
Landauer, Gustav, 121, 124
leaks, leaking. *See* whistleblowing, WikiLeaks
liminality. *See also* borders, 119
Luddites, 34–35, 37
LulzSec, 4, 13, 15, 68, 104
   hacking for fun, 54–55
LulzXmas Stratfor hack, 69

M
Manning, Chelsea Elizabeth
   (née Bradley Edward), 69–70,
   95–97 , 99, 100
Marx, Karl, 3, 22, 109
McChesney, Robert W., 1, 2, 3
McKay, Peter (Canadian
   Defense Minister), 15
metadata, 15–18 , 103
military
   and hackers, 69–70
   in film WarGames, 51–52
   law and use of force, 80
   origins of the internet, 1
   whistleblowing and the, 88,
   94–95
   See also disciplinary power
Millenium (Hakim Bey),

118–20

Mills, C. Wright, 18

modernity , industrial, 75, 78, 81

second, or post-modernism, 94, 108, 118, 120

Monsegur, Hector Xavier. *See* Sabu

moral(s), morality

of hackers, 41–43, 53. *See also* whistleblowing

panic(s), 23, 39

regulation of, 10

Most, Johann, 30

N

Nader, Ralph, 88

Negri, Antonio, 108, 110–111, 129–130

NSA (US National Security Agency), 103

in film portrayal, 57

Snowden revelations on

mass surveillance by, 15–17

TAO (Tailored Access Operations), 132

O

Omega (hacker), 63–64

openness, 107–8

See also commons

organizations, organizational practice, 62

Oxblood Ruffin, 63–64, 79, 98

P

Palmer Raids, 26

Panopticon (Jeremy Bentham's permanent visibility prison), 80, 82, 103

PayPal, 3

peer review, 81

peer-to-peer (P2P) networks, 6, 101, 109 , 110, 116

PGP. *See* Pretty Good Privacy

pharmaceutical industry, 92–93

PIPA (US-Preventing Real Online Threats to ...Intellectual Property Act), 65

piracy, 54, 61, 65, 66, 73, 107, 137n8

Playstation Network hack, 67

Polanyi, Karl, 120

police, 19, 20, 23, 37, 69

post-modernism , 94, 108, 118, 120

anarchism and, 123–124

poststructuralism, 124

potenza (constituent power), 129–30

power

and discipline, 80–81

disciplinary, 80–86

governmentality, legal regimes and, 78–80

Pretty Good Privacy (PGP encryption), 12–13

primitive accumulation, 3

PRISM, 15, 103. *See also* NSA
prison(s), 10, 80, 81, 85, 136
  in film, 48
  hackers in, 13, 68, 101
  whistleblowers in, 93, 97, 99
  See also the Panopticon
privacy, 86
  confidentiality, data
  retention, 84–85
  confidentiality, data
  integrity, 79–80
  disciplinary power and,
  81–82
  hacking and, 47
  invasions, 17–18
  vs. security tradeoff, 18
propaganda
  of the deed, 24, 36
  of the state, 49, 70
property
  intellectual. *See also* SOPA,
  65–66
  rights, as enclosure of the
  mind, 104
Proudhon, Pierre-Joseph, 10,
  123
public interest , 88, 91, 93

R
Ranters (or Diggers), 104
Red Scare(s), 25–27, 38–39
regulation
  academic discipline, 81
  Health Canada de-, 92

of the internet, 35, 75, 80,
  84–86
  state, 10, 100, 108
  revolution, 121
  anarchist social change, 26,
  32, 37–38
  immediatist, 118
  portrayed as conspiracy, 32
Riseup (Networks & Labs), 39,
  134

S
Sabu (Hector Xavier
  Monsegur), 67–68
Scientology, Church of, 50, 51,
  54
Sneakers (film by Phil Alden
  Robinson), 46, 54–55, 57
Snowden, Edward, 15–16,
  102–3
social action, 123–25
  See also direct action
social structures, 37
Sony Electronics, Inc, 67–68
SOPA (US-Stop Online Piracy
  Act), 65–66
Squire, Jo, 2, 4, 5, 8, 135
state
  capital and, 10, 18, 21, 34, 35
  enclosures by, 2–3, 12, 21
  violence and repression, 19,
  24, 26, 36, 72, 86
  surveillance by, 15
  whistleblowing and the, 89, 90,

92–93
See also Canada; FBI; globalization, NSA; PRISM; United
States
Stirner, Max, 121
strain theory, 45
Stratfor hack, 69
strike(s) , 38, 85, 133, 134–35
surveillance
by Canadian state, 15–19
monitoring and disciplinary
power, 80–83
Panopticon, 80
PRISM, 15, 103
society and, 79
See also metadata, NSA
Swordfish (film by Dominic
Sena)
syndicalism, 38, 127, 130–36

T
TAO Communications, 39, 104,
132–36
terrorism, terrorists
anarchists portrayed as, 24,
26, 28, 30, 33, 35
anti-terror panics, 39
hackers portrayed as, 21, 38,
52–53 , 58, 59
'poetic', 117–18
state vs. non-state actors, 36
'war on', 17, 18, 25, 33, 36
Tiqqun. *See* The Invisible
Committee

Toews, Vic (Minister of Public
Safety, Canada), 85
Tor, 79
Toronto, 19, 133, 134
trickster figure, 55

U
Unabomber, 33–35, 114
United Nations Declaration of
Human Rights, 64
United States
State Department, 12–13
whistleblowing in, 87-89

V
V for Vendetta (film by James
McTeigue), 48–49, 53
video games. *See* gaming,
video

W
war
financing of, 70
on terror, 17 , 25, 33, 36
profits vs. public image,
69–70
WarGames (film by Lawrence
Lasker), 45, 51–52, 53, 55
Westboro Baptist Church , 50,
51
whistleblowing, 99–100 , 103
Canadian legal context of,
90–91, 90–92
defined, 87

US history of, 87–89
Wikileaks, 94–95, 100–101
Wikipedia, 66 , 67, 101
Wilson, Cody, 10–15
World Trade Organization,
    demonstrations against, 127
workers' control, 110

See also autonomy
working class (& organizations
    of), 20, 38, 111 , 130–31

Z
Zapatistas, 121–24

zero
books

Contemporary culture has eliminated both the concept of the public and the figure of the intellectual. Former public spaces – both physical and cultural – are now either derelict or colonized by advertising. A cretinous anti-intellectualism presides, cheerled by expensively educated hacks in the pay of multinational corporations who reassure their bored readers that there is no need to rouse themselves from their interpassive stupor. The informal censorship internalized and propagated by the cultural workers of late capitalism generates a banal conformity that the propaganda chiefs of Stalinism could only ever have dreamt of imposing. Zer0 Books knows that another kind of discourse – intellectual without being academic, popular without being populist – is not only possible: it is already flourishing, in the regions beyond the striplit malls of so-called mass media and the neurotically bureaucratic halls of the academy. Zer0 is committed to the idea of publishing as a making public of the intellectual. It is convinced that in the unthinking, blandly consensual culture in which we live, critical and engaged theoretical reflection is more important than ever before.